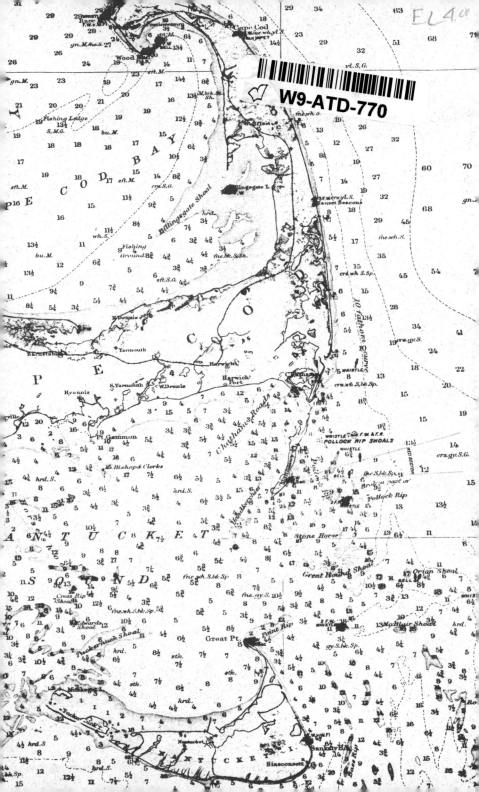

AMERICA'S LANDFALL

The Historic Lighthouses
of
CAPE COD, NANTUCKET &
MARTHA'S VINEYARD

AMERICA'S LANDFALL

———•◆•———

The Historic Lighthouses
of
CAPE COD, NANTUCKET &
MARTHA'S VINEYARD

———•◆•———

D O N A L D W. D A V I D S O N
preface by
J A M E S W A R D H Y L A N D III
President & Founder
The Lighthouse Preservation Society

Cape Cod · Nantucket · Martha's Vineyard
New Bedford · Plymouth

Published by
The Peninsula Press · Cape Cod 02670 USA
www.capecod.net/peninsulapress

First published in 1993 by The Peninsula Press
Library of Congree Catalog Card Number: 96-067225
Davidson, Donald W.
    AMERICA'S LANDFALL: *The Historic Lighthouses of Cape Cod,*
    Nantucket & Martha's Vineyard.
    The Peninsula Press, ©1993.
    Includes index, bibliography, and illustrations.
ISBN: 1-883684-09-9
1. Cape Cod, Nantucket & Martha's Vineyard — Lighthouses.
2. Cape Cod, Nantucket & Martha's Vineyard — History and commerce.
3. Cape Cod, Nantucket & Martha's Vineyard — Geography and geology.

Fourth edition
Manufactured on Cape Cod in the United States of America
4 5 6 7 8 9 10 11 12 13 / 08 07 06 05 04 03 02 01 00 99

GREAT POINT LIGHT
(preceding title page*) with
stood winds and waters for
more than two centuries
before this Nantucket tower
was destroyed. It was then
replicated with funds
sought by the efforts of
Massachusetts Senator
Edward M. Kennedy.*

For my family,
for my friends,
and for all of those
who "must [go] down to the sea in ships,"
their families and their friends as well.

TABLE OF CONTENTS

BRANT POINT LIGHT *has stood atop several towers over the past two centuries. Here its bare, red brick reveals a construction more like the towers at* CAPE COD, GAY HEAD, *and* WEST CHOP.

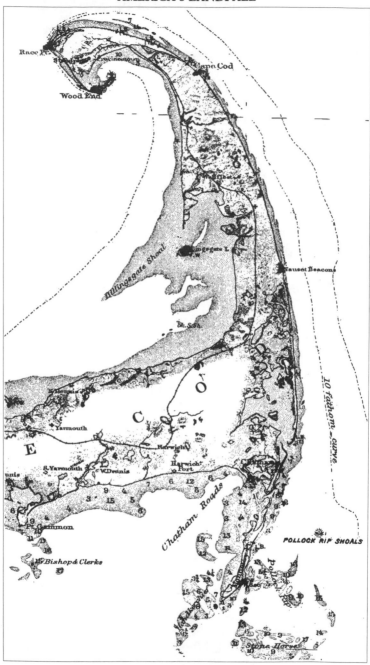

PREFACE

WHO COULD POSSIBLY IMAGINE Cape Cod, Nantucket & Martha's Vineyard without their lighthouses? They have become a symbol for the region. And yet, it was not always so. Although few of those who live beside these waters would willingly part with their beloved lighthouses today, there was a time when these saltwater sentinels were actually hated and despised by a large segment of the population on the Cape & Islands during the late 1700s and early 1800s.

During those years, a large group of otherwise respectable people were engaged in the shipwrecking business. They were called "mooncussers," because they would lure vessels onto the shoals and bars during the nights when there was no moonlight to illuminate the shoreline.

Armed with a betraying "Judas lantern," mooncussers would situate themselves on the shore, directly behind the shallows, then gyrate their lantern in a manner that resembled the sway of a ship's mast lantern. Upon seeing the light, the deceived captain of a passing vessel would steer toward its direction,

THE GENERAL CHART of the Coast No. VII (Cape Ann to Block Island with Georges Bank), *published in November of 1892 by the United States Coast & Geodetic Survey, appears here in edited form to show the outer stretch of the Cape and its shoals. Most of the depth readings have been removed for easier reading; however, those that remain indicate how shallow and treacherous the waters are around the Cape & Islands.*

believing that another ship had found safe waters. Before he knew it, though, he would find himself aground. And if the surf were sufficiently rough, the ship would begin to break up, washing its cargo to shore to be collected by the locals. If the sea were calm, mooncussers were known to row out to the stranded vessel, board her, beat the sailors, and row to shore with the cargo.

When Ralph Waldo Emerson visited Eastham during that period, he found violent opposition to the construction of the Nauset Beach lighthouse, because it "hurt the wrecking business." Emerson saw grim proof that the trade was flourishing when he observed the many unmarked graves in the area. In fact, before a network of aids to navigation was developed in the 1800s, three out of every five New England sailors perished at sea, whether by natural causes or at the hands of their fellow man.

In 1794, a pastor from the lower Cape town of Wellfleet, the Reverend Levi Whitman, out of concern for the lives of those who sailed around Cape Cod sought to have a lighthouse built in North Truro "on the high land . . . near the Clay Pounds," where — at that time — more vessels were wrecked than in many other parts of the Atlantic. His recommendation, together with agitation by the Boston Marine Society, brought about the construction in 1797 of Cape Cod Light, known popularly as the Highland Light.

The first lighthouse to be built on the Cape itself, Highland Light quickly became one of the most important lights in America. It was usually the first landfall seen by navigators bound from Europe to Boston, and — for many years — it was the most powerful beacon in New England.

Many more lighthouses would be constructed by our fledgling government in the years to follow. In 1789, George Washington signed the 9th Act of Congress, which established a system of aids to navigation along this nation's shores. The idea was to build enough lighthouses

to make our coastline safe, and the goal was to erect a beacon every 20 miles or so along the coast so that a ship would never be out of sight of a lighthouse. This was America's first Public Works Act and is considered to be the first great work of the American people.

In those days, major transportation was carried out by ship. Lighthouses, therefore, were vital to protect the commerce and immigration that was the lifeblood of this young country.

As the nation moved into the 1800s, it saw the development of incredible breakthroughs in science and technology. At the start of those years, we knew very little about light magnification, fuels, and the engineering problems involved with the construction of lighthouses in offshore locations, on shifting sands, and on dangerous headlands. The challenges that lighthouse technology posed in that era can be compared to those challenges faced today in the space race. Lighthouses, in fact, were the standard by which nations measured their scientific achievement in those days.

During the 1900s, lighthouses had reached their zenith,

CAPE COD LIGHT *has been depicted in countless etchings, drawings, and photographs throughout the past 200 years; this image appeared in a 19th-century edition of* Harper's New Monthly, *and its details include the steam-operated fog signal to the right. As preparations were made for relocating the tower in the summer of 1996, the Cape Cod National Seashore anticipated even more than the annual two million visitors to this site.*

and then — with the development of new technologies in navigation — started to decline. As the end of this century now approaches, we tend to think of lighthouses romantically. It cannot be denied that these beautiful structures in their picturesque settings possess a certain mystique. The stories of shipwrecks and heroism, of pirates and buried treasure, of love and war that surround many of America's lights simply add to the romance that we all sense about these wonderful places.

I personally know of no other subject in American history that contains such a vast reservoir of folklore and legend. In many ways, lighthouses are to North America what castles are to Europe. Numerous comparisons can be made between these two types of structures, but let it suffice to say they both provide a setting in our respective cultures and literature for adventure, romance, and symbolism.

Like Europe's castles, we also need to preserve this maritime heritage for generations to come. Though lighthouses have long been regarded in song and poetry as immortal beacons, they can no longer be taken for granted. They are becoming an endangered species. While some still send their luminous warnings across the waters, others are succumbing to a relentless barrage of vandalism, decay, and budget cuts, not to mention the constant pounding of wind and rain, sand and surf. And no force is more immediate than simple neglect, a hazard we each have the power to avoid.

For example, a number of lights that have protected the waters surrounding Cape Cod, Nantucket & Martha's Vineyard have found themselves facing the immediate dangers of erosion. The Great Point Light on Nantucket already has fallen into the sea, only to be resurrected through efforts by concerned citizens and government agencies alike. Others since threatened with similar danger attracted attention as well. In time, local groups on the outer Cape found cooperative efforts with the Cape Cod

National Seashore and the Coast Guard to relocate the endangered towers of both Cape Cod and Nauset lights. Hopefully, these aging maritime monuments and others like them will be preserved for future generations.

At one time, nearly forty lighthouses protected the waters surrounding the Cape & Islands. Most certainly, every lighthouse has an interesting story all its own. And though each piece of history remains significant, such individual tales represent only a small portion of America's rich and colorful lighthouse heritage. To that end, the story and images of AMERICA'S LANDFALL together will help cultivate even further your appreciation of our nation's maritime history.

JAMES WARD HYLAND III
President & Founder
THE LIGHTHOUSE PRESERVATION SOCIETY

CHAPTER 1
A NIGHT AT THE LIGHT

EVERYONE LOVES A LIGHTHOUSE, for few other sights on the face of this earth can kindle the spark of imagination as much as does the flash from afar of a beacon through the night. Some see in its silent signal a message of hope unspoken, while others sense in its nightly vigil a knowledge of dangers unseen.

The dream of a lighthouse guiding a ship past this rough fringe of shore around Cape Cod, Nantucket & Martha's Vineyard seems as sound to anyone today as once it did only to locals who had hoped to protect a husband, a son, or a brother at sea. And on nights such as those when the townsfolk tossed in their beds at the sound of a storm, their only comforts often came in knowing that the keeper worked to keep his beacon seen far out to sea.

Out there, the seaman on his watch was vigilant for the "loom" of this one light, the glow it provided on an otherwise dark horizon. Whether low along the sands of Race Point, Billingsgate, and Sandy Neck, or else high above the headlands of Truro, Nantucket, or Martha's Vineyard, these lanterns were all that anyone on deck might be able to recognize from afar as his "landfall."

NOBSKA LIGHT takes on a golden glow when the sun sets beyond the Elizabeth Islands, and its loom scans Vineyard Sound.

In this sense, then, each lighthouse along Cape Cod, Nantucket & Martha's Vineyard would become special and unique to a sailor at sea; however, there are countless other aspects, the result of harbored fantasies and harnessed physics, which make each one just like all the others, for there is something about every lighthouse ever built which exudes an elegance of sorts, and most on shore who see a lighthouse are enchanted by its presence, standing valiantly alone no matter what the skies or seas.

Seldom, though, could simple beauty ever save a ship at sea. Through daylight and through darkness, a lighthouse remains a strikingly poetic design dictated only by the constant need to deter some ever present danger.

"The light-house lamp a few feet distant shone full into my chamber and made it as bright as day," remembered Henry David Thoreau of his stay at Cape Cod Light. "I thought as I lay there, half awake and half asleep, looking upward through the window at the lights above my head, how many sleepless eyes from far out on the Ocean stream — mariners of all nations spinning their yarns through the various watches of the night — were directed toward my couch."

Above him, the isolated beacon in the midst of that

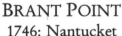

BRANT POINT
1746: Nantucket
WHITE TOWER
Red occulting light every 4 seconds
RANGE: 10 MILES
Clearly visible by the Coast Guard Station at the entrance to the Harbor, the lighthouse can be reached on foot.

From Steamship Wharf, head along Broad Street. After two blocks, go right for another four blocks along South Beach Street until you come to Easton Street. Take your right on Easton, which will lead you to the lighthouse.

For passage to Nantucket, see the *Transportation Appendix.*

19th century night was not the first one this nation had built, nor was it even the first on this Commonwealth's coast. And yet, the wandering visitor to Cape Cod had rightly sensed that this particular lighthouse held some stronger significance than simple romance would allow.

"On studying the map," he had noted long before he ever traveled to Truro on foot, "I saw that there must be an uninterrupted beach on the east or the outside of the forearm of the Cape, more than thirty miles from the general line of the coast, which would afford a good view of the sea."

BRANT POINT LIGHT *has known more than a half dozen incarnations since the very first one was built by the townspeople of Nantucket some thirty years before* CAPE COD *was built upon the mainland. Today's light stands on the edge of the harbor entrance, not far from where an earlier cast iron tower remains at the Coast Guard Station.*

Above the beach to the west, the NANTUCKET CLIFF RANGE LIGHTS *once had guided sailors to safe water.*

But the view he found from these High Lands of Truro was more than just "good." It was a virtual panorama spreading far across the nearby edge of the Atlantic Ocean, one of nature's sterner works of beauty, and once Thoreau had witnessed this for himself, he could

17

BEACH POINT LIGHT *on Barnstable's Sandy Neck (opposite page) once appeared like this and was quite similar to* STAGE HARBOR *in Chatham (below) in shape and fate.*

Decommissioned, their lanternless towers and keepers' dwellings are each now private property: envied by others, but still vulnerable to storms.

literally see what far too many sailors had often discovered all too late; namely, that there was more to be revealed just off these restless shores than any chart at hand might those days explain.

"If the history of this beach could be written from beginning to end, it would be a thrilling page in the history of commerce," Thoreau later wrote, for there between the lighthouse and some deck at the far horizon prevailed a coastal condition so treacherous that during the next half century alone nearly a thousand ships would wreck within the very sight of shore.

"The annals of this voracious beach! Who could write them, unless it were a shipwrecked sailor?" he observed. "Many who have seen it have seen it only in the midst of danger and distress, the last strip of earth which their mortal eyes beheld."

This, then, is the story of why and how these lights had come to be. And of how their time is now upon the verge of passing.

One can only imagine what Thoreau would write today if he were to learn that those ships just beyond the vast horizon are no longer peering toward his couch. For

years after his visit, they listened instead to something called a radio beacon, which sent invisible flashes of its own: four dots, then two dots, a coded abbreviation for Highland Light that said, *HI*. But even that has been replaced by a navigational signal beamed from satellites in orbit overhead.

And what might the late romantic think in learning that the keeper's work is seldom more than that of a handy man, changing light bulbs once a month and cleaning lenses even less. Of all the lighthouses which one time stood along these fabled Cape Cod shores, Cape Cod Light had been the first to get its keeper simply because it had been the first to be built upon the Cape. Then, it became the last in these parts to merit one when all but Boston Light became automated. Today, the latter station on Boston Harbor's Little Brewster Island remains the only lighthouse in America with a "wicky" still in residence.

Somehow, now, the living romance has all but vanished. No longer do the folks in town imagine how the keeper of the light is faring in a storm. No longer do the seamen on their bridges search the far horizon for their landfall on a starless night. And all those here along this shore who yearn to think that somewhere on the ocean stands a sailor on the watch must look beyond the Cape Cod Light to find some common point of focus. ⚓

CHAPTER 2
GENESIS REVISITED

IN THE BEGINNING America was New England, and New England was Cape Cod. On moonless nights, her shore lay dark beneath the flicker of stars; on cloudy nights, her shore lay that much darker still. And when the weather sullied nights with storms from any quadrant, this sand spit and all of its islands lay well hidden as a hazard.

There was no loom from lighthouse lamps, no forlorn moan from foghorns. Not one dull clang from onshore bells tolled through the pitch of darkness. Along this stark and barren shore, not one such aid existed. On lands still bearing native names, like Nauset and Nantucket, no New World needs had yet been found to justify such things. Until such time when names of land and needs of such were known, only fools or fearless men dared venture her dark waters.

By light of day, on the other hand, this Cape & Islands coast seemed so much more attractive. First, as a subject of the Old World's curiosity; then, as an object of its wants. To these waters came the world's most celebrated voyagers with the collective intent of shedding upon the shore some light of their very

THE GURNET LIGHT *displays not only weathered shingles exposed to winter's northeast winds off Cape Cod Bay, but also red-tinted glass in the southeasterly panes of its lantern to warn mariners of hazardous rocky waters in the approach from those degrees of the compass.*

own. Here sailed the cartographer Samuel de Champlain, as well as the adventuring Captain John Smith, and the lesser-known Bartholomew Gosnold, all of whom followed the expeditions of those known to most as little more than "Norsemen."

Whatever their goals and whatever their homeports, their route to this world was by water. Provided with little other choice, these mariners knew what the rest of the world most certainly understood: sailing the open Atlantic was one thing, but piloting near an unknown shore was altogether another. No one yet had maps of

---

THE GURNET
1768: Plymouth
WHITE OCTAGONAL TOWER
Flashes white alternating 7, then 4.5 seconds
RANGE: 16 MILES

Visiting this light takes some doing, but seeing it is simple. The least strenuous forms of visit would be either by properly documented ORV along Duxbury Beach, or by boat from Plymouth, Kingston, or Duxbury Harbors. The option to walk the length of the beach to the Gurnet requires a great deal of stamina and time.

From the Sagamore Bridge at the Cape Cod Canal, take Route 3 north to Exit 10/South Duxbury. Follow Route 3A north, then take a right onto Route 14 into Duxbury Village. Not far past the high school, bear right at the church onto Powder Point Avenue. At the flagpole, bear left and follow the roadway that keeps Snug Harbor on your right. This will lead you directly to the bridge for Duxbury Beach. Cross the bridge; the roadway to the Gurnet begins on the right.

If you prefer just to see the Gurnet Light and nearby Duxbury Bug with binoculars, take Route 44 off Route 3 and head into Plymouth Center. *The Mayflower II* should serve as a good point of reference. The Gurnet is east of the waterfront, and the Duxbury Bug stands between.

For passage, see the *Transportation Appendix.*

Cape Cod's land, and charts of these waters were sketchy at best. Instead, most shipmasters held faith in those seasoned skills which had come from their practice of reading winds, judging currents, and watching the sky for some sign. Yet, aside from some guidance they found in the stars, their passage was surest by daylight; danger remained in the darkness.

THE GURNET LIGHT *was established prior to the American Revolution, and once consisted of twin towers. Only one of these structures remains, but the ramparts of the other is apparent as the base of the observation tower built during World War II. In 1998, the light was relocated away from the eroding shoreline.*

Even the legendary Christopher Columbus, who has never been said to have sailed these particular waters, knew it better to heave-to at night than to approach any landfall past sundown. Though he was born to a family of weavers, perhaps took heed of advice from his Uncle Antonio, who was keeper of the Genoa light, for on the

deck of the *Santa Maria* in the early October evenings of 1492, Columbus bade his men to keep their keenest watch for any sign of land throughout the coming nights. After all, he had calculated that land was nigh, not due west of his Portugal where the Pilgrims would one day first set foot on shore, but southwest of his starting point toward more pacific waters.

Even before he made his legendary landfall, one difference supposedly stood clear. Columbus claimed that he had spotted — four hours before any land — a light, "like a little wax candle rising and falling."

GREAT POINT
1784: Nantucket
WHITE TOWER
Flashes white every 4 seconds;
shows red 84° – 106°
RANGE: 14 MILES
Not easily accessible at the northern-most tip of this fragile barrier beach, the lighthouse can be reached on foot, by private boat, or by properly documented off-road vehicle.

To approach Great Point on land from Nantucket town, travel east on Orange Street to the rotary at Milestone Road and take the Milestone Road less than a half mile, where you should bear left onto Polpis Road.

Continue on Polpis Road about three miles to Wauwinet Road, which bears to the left. Near the restored hotel at Wauwinet, you will come to an information booth and must stop. Only those ORVs with a permit are allowed any further onto the beach, and even that will depend on certain regulations. By foot, the trek through the sand (out and back!) requires a good deal of stamina.

Meanwhile, the lighthouse is visible (best with binoculars) from the port rail of any vessel entering Nantucket Harbor on a clear day; from the starboard rail of a departing vessel.

And the most dramatic views might well be via air.

For passage to Nantucket, see the *Transportation Appendix.*

Later in the darkness of the early morning hours, a sandy cliff along the west horizon shone bright beneath reflections off the moon, and the earlier cries of *Lumbre!* that had heralded the light, became huzzahs of *Tierra!* that harbingered their find. Though it was his long-sought landfall, as well as history's New World, San Salvador was not a coast as complex as any surrounding Cape Cod, Nantucket or the Vineyard.

For one thing, this shoreline to the north had no such lights — real or imagined — to guide a sailor into port or even warn him of some unseen danger. The New World's first coastal light of record would not be lit until the glow that shone forth from Point Allerton, just south of Boston's harbor.

By the time Columbus had reported to Isabella, then set sail back toward Venezuela in 1498, John and Sebastian Cabot were voyaging from Newfoundland down to Virginia. That father and his son both saw firsthand these northern waters rimmed with its risks and haunted with its weather. A generation later, Giovanni da Verrazano would witness the same from the other direction once he first rounded this sandy coastline that Gosnold would name *Cape Cod* and that Champlain would note as *Malle Barre*, the "evil bar." Here, too, on the waters by Nantucket's shoals was the horror of fog that could hug tightly the boards of a deck.

Yet, even in sunshine there were dramatic extremes which sailors who followed in time would face. These differences were so much more than towering headlands above Nobska and tidal marshes alongside Beach Point, so much more than thoroughfares past Chappaquiddick and quiet coves tucked among the Elizabeths, and so much more than soft-hued spits like Billingsgate and shoals that somehow shifted. The Cape & Islands would be known as a coast of sandbars that would wander with the waters and the winds. And no sailor could ever be certain where such shallows might appear.

25

The Native Americans would give these geographic features names as picturesque as the surf that pounds upon them. And though it was any number of men who had taken the time to name them, Nature was the only force diverse enough to lend them such intriguing forms. Naushon and Nauset, Mattapoisett and Cohasset, Monomoy and Sankaty. No mind of any Man could have conjured up the splendors which enticed countless others to approach them at risk. And all of this landfall and water around it was fully the work of the water itself, first in the form of the glaciers.

Lifetimes ago, icesheet upon icesheet plowed down from the distant north and covered this corner of clay. At some parts, the ice measured nearly two miles deep. Harrowing earth, nudging its boulders, and furrowing channels wide and true, they stopped their advance as the climate grew warmer, then receded north covering tracks up with water. Aside from whatever else they had done to this world, they left in their wake this sandy peninsula and its neighboring islands: Cape Cod, Nantucket & Martha's Vineyard, as well as the Elizabeth Islands.

This wake was the waters that sailors must travel; its legacy of land appeared like this: along its easternmost shores, the rising sun lit early the seaward peaks of the High Lands of Truro and of Sankaty Head. Towering above the North Atlantic, they range as the highest visible seamarks from that direction along the Cape & Islands. By night, however, these headlands by themselves serve no better as any aids to navigation than do the south-stretching strands of Monomoy. On the contrary, they long ranked among a countless list of hazards to be noted, and only those who had encountered them could have passed the word of warning on to others. ✝

NAUSET LIGHT *stood directly above the roaring surf of the Cape's Great Outer Beach; however, its site was threatened by the very same waters. With the guidance and cooperation of the Cape Cod National Seashore, the Coast Guard, and local governments, private citizens organized to have the tower and keeper's dwelling moved to a locale not very far away from this original location.*

27

CHAPTER 3
THE BASIC ELEMENTS

ON VIKING CHARTS a thousand years ago, the outer Cape was something they called *Straumey*, a word that meant "an island with strong currents." Those Norsemen might have been the first to mark it so, and yet they surely would not be the last; the holders of the titles to the nearby shores off Chatham had agreed. They were a tribe of Wampanoag Indians who called themselves the Monomoyicks, from their Algonquin word *Munumuhkemoo*, meaning "there is a mighty rush of water."

These Monomoyicks, so it appears, had taken their own name from the waves and the currents and the tides around them much as the land itself called *Monomoy* had been taken from underneath this constant flow of water. Such was the power of water to create an identity for the land, as well as for the people who lived upon it.

In addition, the water throughout the Cape & Islands has always since influenced its weather. Down from the northeast with freezing swirls, the Labrador Current eddies into the Gulf of Maine, the waters that flow into Cape Cod Bay. Up from the southerly shores, much

CAPE COD LIGHT *still stands above the Atlantic as "America's landfall," but its site has changed considerably from the photographs in this chapter. Several of the outbuildings have been removed or relocated, and the tower has been secured.*

warmer waters flow along Martha's Vineyard, then past the island of Nantucket and beyond. These Gulf Stream waters drift from that quadrant of the compass where Columbus first landed. Just as the colder waters wash through Cape Cod Bay, warmer waters race into Buzzards Bay and the sounds of the Vineyard and Nantucket.

Before there ever would be any lights to mark the edges where water touched land at such places as Cuttyhunk Island on the southwestern corner of the Elizabeths, there had only been the light of the sun to illuminate these passages and then to warm the days. Naturally, what the sun had always done to Cape Cod's waters it had also done to its land and the air above. With differing paces, it heated water, land, and air from dawn until the dusk; then, all at once it left them each to cool throughout the dark hours of the night.

The result along the Cape & Islands coast has always meant a range of temperatures among bodies of water and masses of land, forever in a somewhat confusing state of flux. Always trying to even themselves out, they each must contend with the foibles of the others, so currents of

---

CAPE COD/HIGHLAND
1797: North Truro
WHITE TOWER
Flashes white every 5 seconds
RANGE: 23 MILES
One of the most easily accessible stations, the High Lands of Truro can be reached by taking Route 6 past Truro Center to North Truro.

From the highway, turn right onto Highland Road and follow it east to where it intersects with Coast Guard Road to the left and South Highland Road to the right. Turn right, and in less than a tenth of a mile you should see the lighthouse off to your left on Lighthouse Road. Turn left and continue to the small parking lot.

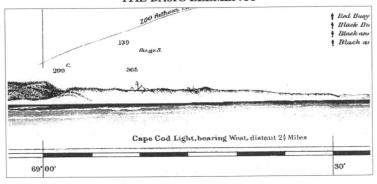

water wash around the land, as well as beneath streams of air, while those same streams of air flow at the same time over the land and the water alike. In places like Nantucket, or Chatham, that interplay of temperatures might create any sort of dirty weather from fog in the summer to flurries of snow thereafter.

Such variations from place to place along this coast and not so far offshore have proved it difficult for even the most experienced of seamen to be able to fathom with any certainty the conditions from day to day. Perhaps if this corner of the continent could be left to contend with just the weather it creates, then sailors might have fewer problems; however, the Cape & Islands' own little relationship among sun and shore and sea is often disrupted — for better or for worse — by whatever flows along the prevailing winds across the continent from the north and west and south, by whatever flows along the Gulf Stream up the eastern seaboard, and by what every shift of wind brings off the water.

In earlier days, these often appeared as tragedy: the howling nor'easter and the raging hurricane, both tending to appear with warning only to those who were aware of their earliest signs. For snow, it was often the look of the

THE GENERAL CHART of the Coast No. VII (Cape Ann to Block Island with Georges Bank), published in November of 1892 by the United States Coast & Geodetic Survey not only provided navigational statistics, but also detailed etchings of selected horizons so that those at sea might best recognize those landfalls critical to their safe passage. As indicated, this one depicts CAPE COD LIGHT from a ship bearing west some 2½ miles off the peninsula.

31

clouds; for wind, the uneasy feel of a stillness, as well as the shape of the seas. And always for both, there was something to be sensed from the smell in the air. Those who would know such things would harken to all their senses, and this is not hard to understand. Either a master knew that, or else he did not, and no lighthouse could offer much help.

SANKATY HEAD LIGHT *shares many of the architectural and geological characteristics as the stations at* GAY HEAD *and* CAPE COD. *Set high atop the edges of fragile headlands, their brick towers each supported a Fresnel lens of the highest order and have been threatened by the constant erosion by the pounding sea.*

All the while, the waves and currents that come from changes in the temperatures of the Cape & Islands air and water have not been the only disturbing ways of the North Atlantic. The points and inlets that jut and break the length of these shores are also the work of lunar tides, those waves worldwide created by the tug of gravity. At the northern end of Monomoy's south island, for example, the land is low and narrow from these tidal overflows. Further south, however, the coastline starts to flare and the beach begins to rise in windswept dunes.

Once the sands have exposed them-

CAPE COD LIGHT *once presided over a substantial site; however, the cliffs in this historic photo have since been worn away by high tides, Atlantic storms, and rain water washing over the edge. Efforts to relocate the light by the National Park Service, the Coast Guard, and a group called "Save Cape Cod Light" revealed that clay is the foundation immediately beneath this tower.*

selves above the surface of the ocean, the way of the winds picks up where the seas leave off. A single grain exposed on a sandbar need only find itself protected on the leeward side of a moonsnail's shell or of a sprouting clump of beach grass and soon a small, but certain mound of sand can then begin to build. In time, this mound of sand drifts higher, only to become the first dune on a beach. This, in turn, will then protect the other sands

GAY HEAD

1798: Gay Head, Martha's Vineyard
RED BRICK TOWER
Flashes alternate white & red every 15 seconds
RANGE: 24 MILES

Though the trip to the lighthouse is not complicated, it remains a relatively long one by car; obviously, longer — out and back — by bicycle. Depending upon your route, the total could range 35 miles. These directions are from Vineyard Haven in Tisbury.

Take Vineyard Haven Road to the west past Lambert's Cove for about 6 miles, where you will approach the fork of North Road (right to Menemsha) and South Road (left to W. Tisbury). Bear left onto South Road.

Continue on South Road for several miles as you pass through the tiny, quaint center of West Tisbury and on through the rocky and rolling farmlands of Chilmark that overlook the vast Atlantic to the south on your left.

At Beetlebung Corner, you will arrive at the center of Chilmark: an intersection of Middle Road to your right, Menemsha Cross Road straight ahead, and the continuation of South Road to your left. Turn left.

Cross the tiny bridge between Stonewall Pond (left) and Nashaquitsa Pond (right) and continue straight ahead. You are still nearly six miles from the lighthouse; however, there will be no doubts when you have arrived at its spectacular height overlooking Vineyard Sound and the Elizabeth Islands along the northerly horizon.

For passage to the Vineyard, see the *Transportation Appendix*.

from wind until the shoal becomes a bar-
rier beach, such as this one now broken off
the coast of Chatham's mainland. There are
others that stretch not so far away: inside
Cape Cod Bay at Sandy Neck; just to the
north of the Cape at Hull, Scituate, and
Duxbury; to the south at Great Point on
Nantucket, then south and west at
Chappaquiddick, down-island on Martha's
Vineyard.

GAY HEAD LIGHT
*here shows a drape over
its lantern to prevent
the rays of the sun from
penetrating the Fresnel
lens and igniting the
lamps in the daytime,
just as a magnifying
glass might do.*

Just offshore from this windswept coastline, the surrounding waters lend no greater comfort. South of
Monomoy Island, for example, stretches Pollock Rip slue,
a confluence of tidal currents from the ocean and the sound
that even scientists of the 19th century had recognized as
being treacherous. "There is no other part of the world,
perhaps," wrote the director of the United States Coast and
Geodetic Survey back in 1869, "where tides of such very

small rise and fall are accompanied by such strong currents running far out to sea."

So for tens of years, those who sailed to and from the waters of the Cape & Islands could only call upon their seafaring intelligence, their coastwise instinct, and their natural intuition to help them pilot vessels safely here from distant ports and then back home again. Basically, through firsthand observations of Cape Cod, Nantucket & Martha's Vineyard, as well as secondhand discussions with other seamen who had experienced still different conditions in these parts, they came to understand in their own sort of way not only the water and the land of the Cape & Islands, but also the weather. In time, they found it worth their while to return. And then, at last, to stay.

CAPE COD LIGHT
once had a Fresnel lens that dwarfed the height of its keeper.

Coming to grips with the very realities which were Cape Cod, Nantucket & Martha's Vineyard demanded an understanding that must begin with the workings of the waters, and that is something that many a landlubber still sometimes fails to understand. Yet, it is those most inclined to turn their faces toward the sun and their backs against the wind who still must learn to respect and appreciate the hazards that once lingered at water's edge, at a time when water's edge was all that America was.

Such is the heritage of Cape Cod & the Islands, and a reason the lighthouse was needed. ⚓

GAY HEAD LIGHT
no longer has either the keeper's house, or the lens depicted on page 35. The lantern and lighting now resemble the present lantern at CAPE COD.

37

CHAPTER 4
CHANGES ON THE HORIZON

GIVEN A GOOD VESSEL upon the open sea, a crew might live forever; however, in waters like those off the Cape & Islands, closed and swift and often quite shallow, the best founded vessel with the ablest of seamen could never expect such good fortune. More often than not in these waters, peril was only a matter of time.

Clearly, then, some sailors were more lucky than others, and that was the best that any crew might hope for. The same might be said of any passenger, which rated — along with any member of the crew — below the value of any cargoes.

After all, much of the passage through earliest routes consisted of seagoing vessels that carried new colonists here, then took back to the Old World ports fish which had been caught in Cape Cod's teeming waters. This was the shimmering wealth from the wilderness, often called "New England's silvermine," and following the word of explorers since gone, fishermen had next become the ones who sailed this wretched shoreline and hoped to wrest some livelihood from its brine.

Neither frightened by seas, nor fear-

CAPE POGUE LIGHT stands at the very tip of Chappaquiddick on the eastern end of Martha's Vineyard, where its site has been "hardened." The light itself is automated, and there is no longer its large Victorian-style keeper's house.

ful of work, these seamen toiled to reach these waters with a purpose. If they knew it not before, then they learned this on the way: Atlantic winds blow hard here from the north, and loud and long they howl out in a storm. Riding heavy winds and rougher seas, they found some times the voyage could be tedious; other times, it

---

CAPE POGUE
1801: Chappaquiddick Island, Martha's Vineyard
WHITE TOWER
Flashes red every 4 seconds
RANGE: 9 MILES

Much like the light at Great Point, this station is not easily reached. Though it can be reached by foot, or by properly-documented off-road vehicle, the lighthouse might be more readily approached by the water. In fact, to reach it by foot or by ORV, you still need to cross Edgartown Harbor via the colorful little "On Time Ferry," then pass through the Cape Pogue Wildlife Refuge.

To do that, take Chappaquiddick Road east from the "On Time Ferry" to Dyke Bridge Road and continue to the lot near the bridge. ORVs must be granted a permit; hikers must follow regulations of the reservation's trustees. Head north along the outer beach; roundtrip from here is close to five miles.

For passage to the Vineyard, see the *Transportation Appendix*.

could destroy their souls. Yet, they also had learned that this coast that compromised the safety of all sailors also inveigled cod to spawn here during winter, when shallow bays were warmer than deeper banks offshore.

A FOG HORN powered by steam added an element of precautionary warning to vessels at sea whenever a beacon could not penetrate the hazards of the weather.

These early settlers were neither Pilgrims, nor Puritans, nor simply colonists; they were fishermen who came to do their business.

These men would be the first to change the landscape of the wilderness, but not with steeples peeking through the treetops. Instead, their seaside skyline rivaled that on shore. In fact, a good many new masts and spars had come from trees along these desolate shores; so, too, had hulls of boats that might be made with ordinary hand tools. With those, they were laying the keels of a rich New England heritage.

Hatchets and axes, handsaws and hammers, adzes and scrapers, chisels and mauls all along the shoreline rang a rhythm resounding in harmony that moved these native woods out to the New World's waters. Though the pine

belt ranged from the maritimes the French called *Arcadia*, down through western Maine and then New Hampshire, there stood timbers aplenty suitable for shaping. The short-needled juniper trees the natives called *hackmatack* grew well in this primeval forest, along with chestnut and spruce, cedar and elm, as well as maple and oak. In time, they all took form as keels and ribs and stems, as well as decks and hulls. The first shapes were often as shallops and scows, local barges and longboats that easily maneuvered through the rivers, coves, and marshes. Other craft were built for coastal travel: ketches and sloops.

Still, more than a hundred years would pass before the Great Outer Beach of Cape Cod bore any lighthouse, though much sooner there would be some lights in waters not so far away. Despite the fishing and coastal trades, yet another generation of sailors would be faced with darkened Cape Cod shores before any ports might show any reliable light at all. Certainly, there were communities where someone had always tried to keep a signal fire of sorts; however, the one which would find official sanction — and a keeper — came just south of the entrance to Boston Harbor with a beacon on Point Allerton just off the beach at Hull. Busy Boston Harbor held the water and the rocks that coursed along its glacial tributaries: the Chelsea and the Malden Rivers, the Island End and the Mystic Rivers, as well as the Neponset and the Charles.

"There are many small islands before Boston, well on to fifty, I believe, between which you sail on to the town," wrote the Dutchman Jaspar Dankers in his 1680 journal. "A high one, or the highest, is the first that you meet. It is twelve miles from the town and has a beacon upon it which you can see from a great distance, for it is in other respects naked and bare." On this head was set

CHATHAM LIGHT *is shown in the left center of this photograph with its lone south tower. A great deal of the waterfront in the lower right has been washed away since the late 1980s. Very close inspection of the upper right hand corner of this photo reveals the light station at* STAGE HARBOR *on the west side of that harbor's entrance into Nantucket Sound.*

43

Point Allerton light, commissioned by 1673 and tended by Capt. James Oliver.

Though it might have been little more than a lighted pole, it possibly resembled the *vippefyr* that was invented by Jens Pedersen Groves and was first used along the Danish coast as early as 1624. Its design was very simple: across a high-set fulcrum point, a levered pole was placed. Upon one end of the lever was an open basket for lighted coals; upon the other, a weight to raise the glowing basket, or lower it for stoking.

As primitive as the light at Point Allerton may have been, it did serve to some a promise; however, it would be a long time before a lighthouse changed the shape of skylines any further, for years would pass before any sort of trade within the colonies might justify the expense of putting up such lights. Though the beacon at Point Allerton may not have been bright, it stood out as a first along this darkened coast.

In the years before, the explorers and the colonists already had seen the need for such. In November of 1620, the master of the *Mayflower* had scuttled plans to skirt the shoals that rimmed Cape Cod and Nantucket. Battered for sixty-five storm-tossed days at sea, pushed northward off

CHATHAM
1808: Chatham Harbor
WHITE TOWER
Flashes white twice every 10 seconds
RANGE: 28 MILES

This is probably the easiest lighthouse to visit throughout the Cape & Islands. Follow Main Street in Chatham to its easternmost end, then turn right at the STOP sign onto Shore Road. From there, the station is less than a mile ahead on your right with a parking lot directly across the street. The site overlooks the dramatic break in North Beach, which has drastically altered the contour of the harbor and its adjacent shores.

course by an unknown force that others would later name the Gulf Stream, and sitting in tricky winds some five miles off the Cape, Christopher Jones and his *Mayflower* faced conditions off Monomoy that made him seek protected waters.

These Pilgrims passed by shores where, in years to come, great beams of light would mark the way at Monomoy and Chatham; north at Nauset; along the

CHATHAM LIGHT originally had twin towers built high above Chatham Harbor. This second set was not the only pair around the Cape & Islands. THE GURNET *once was marked by two;* NAUSET *even had three. Eventually, these Chatham towers were replaced two of cast iron.*

High Lands, and around Race Point. Inside the shelter of Cape Cod Bay, more lights eventually would be set around the shoreline at Provincetown's Wood End and closer by the harbor's mouth at Long Point.

But none of those existed as the *Mayflower* sought refuge at Provincetown before Master Jones decided to leave his passengers with little or no choice at Plimoth. "As one small candle can light a thousand," wrote Governor Bradford in the years to follow, "so the light here kindled hath shone unto many, yea in some sort to a whole nation." ⚓

CHAPTER 5
THE DANGERS OF DEBT

THE WORDS MIGHT HAVE BEEN A PORTEND of beacons and lighthouses to come; however, Bradford had described the tiny coastal plantation that alone would remain without any lighthouse for another century and a half.

The primary purpose of a lighthouse, after all, was not simply to save the lives of sailors and of passengers. Its purpose was first to ensure arrival of a merchant's shipment of goods, and these were something the simple settlers were certain not to have. In other settlements, then, harbor lights first appeared to guide safe passage into more significant shipping ports; other coastal lights marked hazards or distinguished an otherwise featureless landfall; and more than a few pairs of range lights were placed in such a way that a pilot might verify his position in a channel by aligning one beacon directly in front of another, such as at South Hyannis.

Most, if not all, of these would be built by merchants, at first, to save the ships and their cargoes. The value placed on these was more often than not far greater than any value that might have been placed on either the life, or the limbs of people aboard any vessel. After all, the master of a ship

RACE POINT LIGHT *still shines from its tower amongst the dunes of the Province Lands. Though its site has changed some since this archival photo, it continues to provide reliable guidance for small boaters rounding the treacherous race.*

was the only one aboard with any direct connection to these monied men who dealt in commerce. Sometimes a part owner, the master was responsible for the navigation of the vessel and the conducting of any business during transit, as well as the safe transport and delivery of cargo. Still, he was but one soul; if he could not keep his ship afloat to deliver the goods, then he was of no greater use than any one of his subordinates might have been. In that little wooden world, everyone else seemed expendable.

SCITUATE HARBOR LIGHT has a fluted, octagonal tower with an unusual birdcage lantern that ranges above the barrier beach between the harbor and the outer waters of Cape Cod Bay.

Below the master ranked the mates, the carpenter, and an able seaman or two. Sometimes there were others, quite possibly just ordinary seamen who were learning the ropes, and not one of them

SCITUATE HARBOR
1812: Cedar Point
LIGHT GREEN BRICK TOWER
Flashes white with red sector
RANGE: 16 MILES

Because this lighthouse is only fifteen minutes or so by car from both the Gurnet to the south, or Minots Ledge to the north, you might do best to plan to see them all in the same drive. Of the three, Scituate Light has the easiest access. The arrow on the thumbnail map is not misplaced; it simply indicates the approximate site of Scituate in relation to the other landmarks that have been indicated.

From your visit to the Gurnet, take Route 3A north. Bear left as 3A joins Route 139 briefly through Marshfield, then bear right less than a mile later as 3A continues on its own without Route 139. Stay on 3A until it intersects with Route 123, then turn right onto 123 into Scituate center.

Follow the main street through town, where you can see the lighthouse across from the town pier on the right. Just beyond the pier, bear left on Beaver Dam Road and take the right at the traffic light. As you follow this road, you'll continue to see the light as you make your way to its parking lot.

was destined to become wealthy; at least, not within legal bounds. Above them ranked the master, who often ruled with the temper of a tyrant; beneath them rolled the oceans of the world. As the adage said: "Those who would go to the sea for pleasure would go to hell for pastime."

Seldom, if ever, did the wages match the task, but a good many sailors had nowhere else to work. Some had been taken aboard against their very wishes, and others had sought some refuge from the law. In the eyes of the merchants, then, these souls were clearly a worthless lot. Certainly they were worth a lot less to the monied class than was any cargo, or even the ship upon which these mariners sailed. Any expenses to build a lighthouse could only be justified in terms of the value of the goods. To merchants, the darkness presented no mortal danger; the danger in the darkness could mean debt. Mooncussers underscored that, as did colonial governments.

The members of this first group were nothing less than land pirates who did whatever they might to lure into shallows and onto the shores those ships richly burdened with goods. Without any beacon to warn of danger, a master at sea might mistake a light along the coastline as either some indication of landfall, or else of another ship with bearings more true. Too many times,

RACE POINT
1816: Provincetown
WHITE TOWER
Flashes white every 10 seconds
RANGE: 16 MILES
Though the light is visible from your car in the lot by the Coast Guard Station, you will still need to take a healthy hike through the sand for any closer look.

Follow Route 6 all the way to Provincetown, then take a right onto Race Point Road at the stoplight. Follow to the end, where the lighthouse should be visible to the west and south.

however, it turned out to be the work of a group of mooncussers, so named because they cursed those nights when the light of the moon prevented their deadly deeds.

Sometimes they mounted a lantern atop a cattle yoke, then led the plodding beast along the beach. Seen from a distance, this slowly moving light, pitching and yawing through the dark, might be viewed as a ship making deliberate headway. Other times, the mooncussers placed a light high on a pole, then strolled the shoreline just as slowly. A well-meaning master might be lured aground, his ship might be battered to pieces by breakers, and his cargo washed ashore. A few on land might try to rescue sailors, but more went for the goods.

In the 17th century, the colonies passed laws that any wreck be noted at once to the town clerk so that the ship and its cargo could be salvaged. But there was more profit in keeping mum, and the promise of silence was allied to darkness. So strong was the bond that it has long been thought that mooncussers, wreckers, and the communities which found profit from their crimes delayed the construction of lights as late as the mid-19th century. Given the pace at which the lighthouse establishment grew, perhaps there is truth in that thought. 🔱

RACE POINT LIGHT relied upon the same basic principles as other lights in the area. A close look at the white tower shows the shadow of the grounding cable that led down from the lightning rod into the ground.

CHAPTER 6
CROSSROADS

BY THE EARLY 19TH CENTURY, merchants on Cape Cod, Nantucket & Martha's Vineyard were trying to protect their shipments of goods. One by one, ports were emerging through which they could ship their cargoes, and villages continued to emerge along waters that provided access: Wellfleet, Bass River, Hyannis Port. Small and scattered communities, not every one of them necessarily had anything to trade or sell to others; nonetheless, they did need certain goods. Roads among them all were rough and rugged, too slow and much too difficult for moving merchandise. Almost naturally, the smaller boats the local shipwrights made were employed for coastal trade among these tiny towns. Before long, the enterprising merchants with European ties well understood the benefit of routing goods into and out of larger, central harbors, and so did nearby businessmen. After all, some guarantee of safe passage into a port would not only attract the seafaring ships, but also the coastal boats, as well as all the onshore spending that surrounds such activity.

Boston became the first of the colonies to mark the way to its

TARPAULIN COVE LIGHT overlooks the waters where British vessels moored while plundering coasters up and down the Vineyard Sound. The original tower shared its site with a tavern, and the keeper tended both.

harbor. Not far behind its progress with the light at Point Allerton, they set a tower upon one of the Brewster Islands at the easternmost edge of the harbor in 1716. In trying to move cargo both safely and swiftly, any sort of a lighthouse might surely be better than none at all.

The Boston Light was built much as the local boats had been, by local workmen using whatever tools and whatever materials were readily at hand. In this case, local stones and timbers were formed into the shape of a tapered tower: the higher, the better with the stone to keep it stable. Then it was topped with a lantern room that held either candles or lamps. When completed and lighted, it was the first lighthouse in the New World.

Between that time and the forming of a government for the United States of America in 1789, twelve more lighthouses would be built at other prospering ports throughout the colonies; two of those would follow the war for independence. Still, most

POINT GAMMON LIGHT *retains an architecture as distinct as* SCITUATE *or of* CLEVELAND LEDGE. *Its narrow-windowed upper tower rests upon a pedestal of stone.*

POINT GAMMON
1816: West Yarmouth
FIELDSTONE TOWER
Fixed white
RANGE: 13 MILES

Privately owned, this restored light cannot be reached without special permission (or else trespassing). A view is possible, though, with binoculars from the port rail of any vessel leaving Hyannis Harbor, or with binoculars from a vantage point on the breakwater at the entrance to the harbor.

Perhaps the best view is by private boat; however, the waters south of Point Gammon contain countless submerged rocks that are a hazard to navigation.

For commercial passage through Hyannis Harbor, see the *Transportation Appendix*.

of the colonial coastline remained officially dark for yet another generation after the light was put up in Boston Harbor. Nantucket would build the next.

When Nantucket finally set its light upon Brant Point at the entrance to the harbor on the protected, northern shore of the island in 1746, it was not an especially sophisticated station: a short wooden tower with its beacon on top. From the outset, Brant Point Light remained the responsibility of island shipowners who had managed not only to propose the project at the Town Meeting of January 24th, but also to have it completed by the scheduled gathering of April 28th.

Two lights then marked New England's coast, but two lights did not a safe world make, and few things were more treacherous to a ship than what awaited south of Nantucket. In time, the shipping world would come to refer to the area simply as "The Crossroads," where ships from Europe, Canada, New York, Norfolk, Baltimore, and Philadelphia would pass each other in search of their own destinations.

Not unlike the open Atlantic, this area south of the Cape & Islands remained a vast and trackless ocean. Yet, here sat a somewhat greater hazard in the form of inscrutable fog. Perhaps one of the foggiest areas along the entire eastern seaboard, the dirty weather and congested

TARPAULIN COVE
1817: Naushon Island,
The Elizabeth Islands
WHITE TOWER
Flashes white every 6 seconds
RANGE: 9 MILES
This station has long been anchorage for boaters daysailing or cruising the waters throughout the Cape & Islands.

For the scheduled passage through Vineyard Sound, see the *Transportation Appendix*.

shipping of "The Crossroads" together turned this spot on every master's chart into a dreaded graveyard of ships.

The darkness and fog were responsible for the death of many who tried sailing past the Great Outer Beach; "The Cross-roads" proved a deadly rival, for the area never provided what any would consider

THE AIR VENT *atop the lantern was essential for removing smoke and fumes that endangered the keeper. This photo shows the relative size of the vent under repair at on the observation deck at* MINOTS LEDGE.

"ideal" shipping weather. Calm, clear days were few. When the weather was clear, the seas would be rough. When the air was calm, fog would set in as a close and lasting blanket folded tight against the cold North Atlantic's seas.

Shipmasters had another route, although it still proved tricky. To avoid "The Crossroads," they navigated the shallow rip between Monomoy and Great Point. Once through, they passed westerly into shallow, but protected waters: first Nantucket Sound, into Vineyard Sound, then across Block Island, and on through Long Island Sound, clear down to the Hudson. Later, lighthouses and lightships would show the way. Until then, the route remained touch and go.

On land, meanwhile, it was fire — an always present lighthouse danger right up until very recent years — that would greatly damage the original two structures that had stood at Boston and Brant Point. In 1751, flames gutted the rubble Boston Light of all its wooden parts, especially its staircase and its decks, so while repairs were made a temporary beacon was set atop a spar not very far away. A similar fate befell the Brant Point Light in 1758; however, the next one built would be only the second of perhaps as many as nine reincarnations of the original tower that had been placed on Brant Point. Even today, its reputation as being the lowest-level lighthouse in New England stands alongside its reputation as the one lighthouse that has most often been reconstructed.

In 1769 upon Plymouth's Gurnet Point along the western shore of Cape Cod Bay another light was set. Unlike other stations that showed some kind of tower structure, the lighthouse at The Gurnet was truly more a house in shape. Not especially large, the squat rectangular building atop the northern entrance to Plymouth Harbor was as tall as it was long: twenty feet in both directions and sitting fifteen feet wide. At each end of the roof was a lantern, neither of which had lamps that shone with any

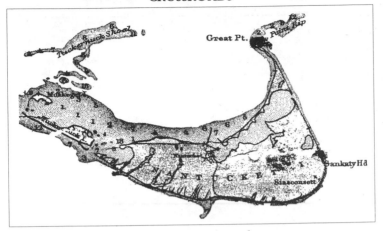

remarkable brilliance. It was, nonetheless, a lighthouse.

Thus, three of America's eleven original lighthouses in place at the outset of the Revolutionary War, were along the waters of the Cape & Islands when the British tried to control the commerce of the colonies. At Brant Point Light on Nantucket, where its people and the British had agreed to a separate peace, the tower rebuilt in 1759 blew over in 1774; at Boston Light, colonial troops dismantled the lantern in 1775 so that it could not aid the British, and the redcoats responded by blowing it up altogether in 1776; and at The Gurnet, a ball from a cannon in an offshore skirmish landed on the light, but never diminished the lantern.

NANTUCKET ISLAND is the nearest point of land to "The Crossroads," where many a ship has met its fate. Geologically, Great Point is an extension of the same beach that begins at Race Point on the Cape and continues south along the Great Outer Beach and Monomoy Island.

The year after the war was over, Massachusetts built two more lighthouses on her own. One was placed in 1784 across the water from Monomoy Island at Great Point on nearby Nantucket. From there, the beacon could guide ships safely past the rips and shoals into Nantucket Sound. Great Point would be among the last of those lighthouses built before the new federal government took over their administration. ⚲

CHAPTER 7
CHANGING WATCH

IN WINTERTIME, this curving Cape & Islands coast can seem a single element as sea and shore together share a less than friendly hue. Sometimes the wrackstrewn beach shows a hard sepulchral face all cracked with shadows holding onto snow, while winds blast past the grim-visaged sea that nudges at its side. No less somber than the sand's sullen site, the water insists on its own leaden look, tempered at times by a flash of sunlight and crested with white foam.

Other days in winter, this same locale may just as soon seem innocent, quiet and still beneath a newfallen snow that has drifted on beaches, settled on boulders, and blanketed bays bound by ice. For a while, at least, nothing might ever seem able to move, but little has been changed underneath, where sandbars and shoals seen in summer still threaten all hulls that sail near. Even in moments of unblemished beauty, each sight by itself could give shivers to sailors who moved through these waters with canvas and wood.

All in all at the threshold of the 19th century, there were far more sites like

WEST CHOP LIGHT *is one of the few automated lights whose site remains much as it did when it last required a resident keeper. Among the outbuildings shown here is the fog signal in the building by the driveway, as well as two dwellings for keepers.*

these along the wavewashed edge of Cape Cod, Nantucket & Martha's Vineyard than any ship's master might ever avoid, and each would approach them with fear in his heart. These were not sailors beguiled by such beauty or lured by dame Nature's more sirenesque charms; however, often they found themselves suddenly here and wanting to be someplace else.

Many more years would pass before most such dangers along these hostile shores could be properly posted, marked with a warning that alerted all ships of the perils awaiting nearby. Until there was any central authority to determine these threats, to recommend the building of some sort of lighthouse, and to pay for the efforts involved, most of the beacons along this horizon still remained the projects of commercial interests hoping to attract ships into one budding port or another.

WEST CHOP LIGHT
is a whitewashed, brick tower rising high over the Vineyard Sound, where it shares a panorama with NOBSKA, EAST CHOP, *and* CAPE POGUE.

With the government of the United States of America at last beginning to take on some shape, however, the responsibility for building and maintaining lighthouses, as well as all other

WEST CHOP
1818: Vineyard Haven, Martha's Vineyard
WHITE TOWER
White occulting light every 4 seconds; shows red 281° - 331°
RANGE: 15 MILES

Visible from the starboard rail of any vessel crossing Vineyard Sound bound for either Vineyard Haven or Oak Bluffs, the lighthouse might be overlooked at its perch amidst the island homes. Still, it can be reached rather easily from land by following Vineyard Haven's Main Street/West Chop Road almost two miles north.

For passage to the Vineyard, see the *Transportation Appendix*.

aids to navigation finally held out the promise of some uniformity under the new federal government. In 1789, each of the local communities and colonies which had built the original lighthouses gave up control of those existing ones, along with the control over the others then being built. Viewed as an aspect of shipping and commerce, these and all others would

WEST CHOP LIGHT *beams from a Fresnel lens within its original lantern room.* be overseen by the Department of the Treasury for more than the next hundred years.

At first, they were personally administered by Alexander Hamilton before he relinquished control in 1792 to

BIRD ISLAND
1819: Buzzards Bay, Marion
WHITE TOWER
Flashes white
RANGE: 10 MILES

Planning a trip to see this light should probably include a trip to the lighthouse at Ned Point only ten minutes away; another twenty minutes will lead you to the two lights at New Bedford harbor. Follow Route 6 west and go off-Cape through Wareham center. Beyond Wareham center, take a left off Main Street onto Marion Road, which is still Route 6. About five miles down the road, take a left at the lights onto Point Road. This will wind another four miles until it ends at the Kittansett Club, which is private property. There is a small, gravel turnaround from which you can clearly see the light out on Bird Island.

the Commissioner of Revenue, whose responsibilities included the collection of customs fees at every port. These lighthouses throughout America numbered only 15. For the next 30 years or so, the control of the system passed between the Commissioners of Revenue and the Secretaries of the Treasury until the superintendency of all lighthouses fell at last in 1820 to the Office of the Fifth Auditor of the Treasury.

BIRD ISLAND LIGHT *sits off the western shoreline of Buzzards Bay, not far off Marion's waterfront. At the right, the pyramid-shaped outbuilding held the fog bells and signals; between the bell and fog towers stands the oil shed.*

By that time, the War of 1812 had been waged, partly in pursuit of neutral shipping rights for American vessels while France and England engaged in hostilities of their own. By then, too, the number of lighthouses had increased dramatically to include at least thirty others.

Meanwhile, the idea of a canal cutting through the sands of Cape Cod to avoid a treacherous trip around the peninsula remained little more than a seaman's pipedream. In fact, the busiest waters in all the world beyond the English Channel were then within the sounds bounded by the light stations at Cape Pogue on Chappaquiddick Island on the eastern end of Martha's Vineyard; at West Chop not far

away in Holmes Hole (later known as Vineyard Haven);
at Tarpaulin Cove on Naushon Island in the group that
Gosnold had named the Elizabeths; and at Gay Head on
the western end of the Vineyard.

Vessels heading east and north through Nantucket
Sound would drop anchor off the Vineyard to await the
most favorable weather conditions; ships heading toward
the other direction would gain added speed by riding the
tides and the currents through Vineyard Sound, on into
the adjoining waters that were noted on charts as Block
Island Sound.

So there all the lights were indeed keenly watched,
and poor lights could cost someone dearly. In short, the
safe passage for most of the commerce surrounding this
young nation fell primarily to the office of an assiduous
bookkeeper named Stephen Pleasonton, who had accepted
— along with his more customary clerical tasks — control
over these aids to navigation. Unfortunately, his overrid-
ing concern for economic numbers would reign for more
than thirty years.

Represented at the local levels by the Collectors of
Customs, who often held their own local titles as
Superintendents of Lights, Pleasonton provided rather
strict, unimaginative guidelines that allowed his subordinates to administer virtually every local matter that might
arise, whether that was choosing lighthouse sites and

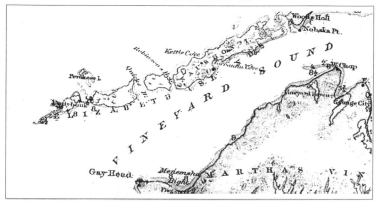

buying land, or issuing construction contracts, then overseeing the work. Though the Secretary of the Treasury officially appointed every lighthouse keeper, they also were generally picked by the local people.

Even so, the Secretary of the Treasury seldom had any more knowledge of their qualifications, or of lighthouse technology, or even of simple station maintenance than did the Fifth Auditor, who seemed more often than not to possess no such knowledge whatsoever. In fact, the closest administrative associate with any understanding remotely related to such maritime matters was a retired captain named Winslow Lewis, himself a Cape Cod native from Wellfleet, whose affiliation with Pleasonton is said to have hindered the whole operation of the lighthouse system much more than it ever helped. The Fifth Auditor, meanwhile, remained little more than a diligent clerk who accepted the word of his local collectors, each of whom received as a salary a percentage of whatever money might be spent upon the lighthouses within their separate jurisdictions. 🕯

VINEYARD SOUND once was bounded by no less than seven lighthouses, including six marked here: CUTTYHUNK *and* GAY HEAD *on the west;* TARPAULIN COVE *in the center; then* NOBSKA, WEST CHOP, *and* EAST CHOP *at the east.*

CHAPTER 8
UPON THESE SANDS

THAT IS NOT TO SAY that other customs officials did not feel more noble obligations. Sometimes sailing and occasionally trekking to some otherwise unreachable extremes of the Cape & Islands, they sought to place daymarks and beacons where they might most be needed.

On occasion, these newly-chosen locations for lighthouses were so remote that no one had yet chosen to settle. That meant that a lighthouse would have to be built either from nearby wood or stone, or else from whatever materials might be shipped or hauled away into this nearby coastal wilderness.

As had been the case in building ships, the people who built the lighthouses did their best with whatever substance seemed available. Since the building of the first beacon upon Point Allerton and the tower in Boston Harbor, the differences through the years among construction techniques, as well as among lighthouse designs closely followed the other evolutions within the nation's growth. Thus, the lighthouse system flourished with the work of those who built towers of wood where they had to, or rubble where they had it.

MONOMOY POINT LIGHT *had been built close to the beach, but dunes that formed later, as well as shoals along the shore, together created a greater distance between the station and the water's treacherous edge.*

Still, regardless of whether such towers would be built out of wood, of rubble, of brick, or — in years still to come — out of concrete or iron pre-cast, the concern among mariners had always remained from the first that the light should be clearly visible. This demanded particular attention to two factors: that the lighthouse be high enough for its lantern to be seen as far as it might out to sea; and that the lighthouse be strong enough not be toppled easily by water or by wind. These concerns of the mariners, though, were not always foremost among Pleasonton, Lewis, and others beneath them, whose untimely practice of politics did often endanger the safety of ships and the lives of those sailors at sea.

Perhaps it took a full generation of questionable policies to reveal any possible pattern of political problems, because by 1838 the Congress had become somewhat suspicious as to whether the Treasury's siting of lighthouses, along with its budgeting, bidding, and spending procedures might not be serving the best interests of America's commerce.

Since the start of the Pleasonton superintendency, yet another forty-three lighthouses had been built along New England's waters, providing this stretch of northeast coastline with nearly half of all the nation's lighthouse stations. Despite that growth — or perhaps because of it — the Congress asked that the Navy Department inspect

BILLINGSGATE
1822: Wellfleet
RED BRICK TOWER
Fixed white
RANGE: 12 MILES

Both Billingsgate Island and the lighthouse that once stood upon it have long since been destroyed by the sea. Last seen around 1922, the station no longer is visible. Pieces of the rock foundation do show themselves, now and then, when the bar is exposed.

each of the nation's lights. Among the less-than-glowing conclusions of that investigation was the disturbing condition of all too many lighthouse structures, let alone their lanterns.

BILLINGSGATE LIGHT *had been supported upon this square, brick tower that stood at the entrance to Wellfleet Harbor. Clearly, this historic photograph depicts the separation of the light from the keeper's dwelling.*

Out here on Cape Cod, the twin towers built at Chatham Harbor in 1808 were typical of several problems that stemmed from local oversight. The first problem was a matter of construction. Planned and designed as two towers of stone, both had been built instead out of wood for no other reason except for the fact that no one could find enough suitable stones along the outer Cape to follow the contract as signed.

"Stones are very rare on the Cape," observed Thoreau. "I saw a very few small stones used for pavements and for bank walls, in one or two places in my walk, but they are so scarce, that, as I was informed, vessels have been forbidden to take them from the beach for ballast."

Wood, on the other hand, was plentiful for two towers.

71

The second problem was simply a matter of numbers. There were two towers built at Chatham Harbor to prevent a lone tower from being mistaken for Cape Cod Light, not too far north along the same Great Outer Beach. The two towers at the Chatham station were not unique, for there were already twin towers north of Boston Harbor built on Thachers Island at Cape Ann, as well as twin towers on Bakers Island in Salem Harbor. In addition, there were the two lights at The Gurnet on the bay in Plymouth.

NAUSET LIGHT, not surrounded by any trees in this archival photograph, displays the more classic architectural styles that Americans put into the pre-fabricated towers: the iron braces below the lantern deck, as well as Victorian arches over the windows were as much decorative as functional.

This multiple tower situation, however, finally reached a point worth questioning on Cape Cod when the three towers of Nauset Beach Light were aligned only a hundred and fifty feet apart. Situated in the town of Eastham, between Truro and Chatham,

NAUSET
1823: Eastham
BANDED TOWER: RED TOP/WHITE BOTTOM
Alternates flashing red, then white at 10 second intervals
RANGE: 23 MILES

This is one of the most popular sites for amateur photographers, because they come across the light more by happenstance than by plan.

Take Route 6 to the National Seashore Visitor Center and turn right at the stop light. Follow Nauset Road as it gently winds and curves leftward about a mile and a half before meeting with Cable Road. Turn right onto Cable Road.

Nauset Light was originally built as three towers that each stood fifteen feet tall. Known as the "Three Sisters," they stand reconstructed along the north side Cable Road; clearly, Nauset Light stands with its own distinctive tower not far away toward the east.

the "Three Sisters" were meant to avoid being confused with the Cape Cod Light to their north and the twin lights of Chatham Harbor to the south. And though it may have been another instance where some local mind had found there was a profit in such a duplicate plan, the Navy inspector thought it was a clear case of this Cape Cod coastline's "overlighting."

If both quality and quantity of lighthouse towers were the first two of the problems which Chatham Harbor typified, then the third was no less simply another case of someone's poor judgment: this time in the matter of siting, as the merciless Atlantic devoured the coastline from under the towers and forced their eventual relocation back from the precipice by 1878.

Already, that had happened at the Cape Cod Light at Truro, when the original thirty-foot tower built in 1797 was replaced altogether less than fifty years later with the one which to this day still stands.

"It rises one hundred and ten feet above its immediate base, or about one hundred and twenty-three feet above mean low water," Thoreau explained after taking the

---

MONOMOY POINT
1823: South Monomoy Island, Chatham
RED IRON TOWER
Fixed white
RANGE: 11 MILES

Monomoy has long been a spit of land whose shape and size change at the whim of the winds and tides. That's why the shipmasters desperately needed a lighthouse there; that's also why it's impossible to approach by land. The south island can be reached with a small craft from Chatham or Harwich; however, the Cape Cod Museum of Natural History does schedule frequent trips. In 1988, the Lighthouse Preservation Society initiated the restoration of the lighthouse and station.

For passage to Monomoy, see the *Transportation Appendix*.

measures on his own. "The mixed sand and clay lay at an angle of forty degrees with the horizon, where I measured it, but the clay is generally much steeper. No cow or hen ever gets down it. Half a mile farther south the bank is fifteen or twenty-five feet higher, and that appeared to be the highest land in North Truro. Even this vast clay is fast wearing away. Small streams of water trickling down it at intervals of two and three rods, have left the intermediate clay in the form of steep Gothic roofs fifty feet high or more, the ridges as sharp and rugged-looking as rocks; in one place the bank is curiously easten out in the form of a large semi-circular crater."

Clearly, the problem had not been so much the construction as it was the selection of the original site above the surf.

"According to the light-house keeper," said Thoreau, "the Cape is wasting here on both sides, though most on the eastern. In some places it has lost many rods within the last year, and, erelong, the lighthouse must be moved. We calculated, *from his data*, how soon the Cape would be worn away at this point, 'for,' said he, 'I can remember sixty years back.' We were even more surprised at this last announcement — that is, at the slow waste of life and energy in our informant, for we had taken him to be not more than forty — than at the rapid wasting of the Cape, and we thought that he stood a fair chance to outlive the former.

"Between this October and June of the next year," he wrote, "I found that the bank had lost about forty feet in one place, opposite the light-house, and it was cracked more than forty feet farther from the edge. But I judged that it was not wearing away here at the rate of more than six feet annually. Any conclusions drawn from the observations of a few years, or one generation only, are likely to prove false, and the Cape may balk expectation by its durability," Thoreau added.

"One old inhabitant told us that when the light-house

"THE THREE SISTERS" *(pictured above and below) once were aligned along the crest of the berm at Nauset Beach to signal the landfall until they were deemed to be "over-lighting" and replaced with a single tower.* was built, in 1798, it was calculated that it would stand forty-five years, allowing the bank to waste one length of fence each year, 'but,' said he, 'there it is' (or rather another near the same site, about twenty rods from the edge of the bank)."

Were Thoreau alive today, he would appreciate the energies of both the Atlantic and the local citizens alike as they confront each other for possession of the Cape Cod and the Nauset lights. At each station, the Atlantic has been rapidly eroding the Great Outer Beach, and private groups have worked with the Cape Cod National Seashore and the Coast Guard to relocate the towers to safer, higher grounds as near as possible to the original sites. Time quickly became of the essence, for a certain amount of ground was necessary for heavy equipment to remove the pre-fabri-

cated Nauset tower and the original brick Cape Cod structure.

The majestic tower that is Cape Cod Light, much like the ones at Nantucket Island's Sankaty Head and Gay Head on the Vineyard, serves well as a model of a coastal light's tower construction. From the top of its cap to the mark of mean low tide on the Great Outer Beach below, the full height above sea level is sufficient to allow its beacon to be seen far enough at sea to prevent mariners from stranding their vessels along those shifting shoals. It was that specific distance beyond the Cape's particular dangers which helped to determine the height of Cape Cod Light.

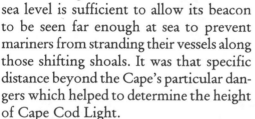

Lighthouse engineers call this distance at sea the *geographic range* of the light; that is, the visibility which the curvature of the earth will allow between the light itself and the eye of an observer out beyond the danger. At the time of the building of the second tower, an observer was considered to be on a ship's deck some fifteen feet above the water; today, he is considered to be on a ship's bridge, another twenty-five feet higher. ☀

"THE THREE SISTERS," *once replaced, were separated and used as private buildings; however, they have been restored recently by the Cape Cod National Seashore and reunited not far from their original location.*

Meanwhile, the NAUSET LIGHT *which replaced them has been relocated to a safer site back from the cliffs.*

CHAPTER 9
FORM AND FUNCTION

HIGH ENOUGH to be seen and far enough back to be safe from the seas, Cape Cod Light has always exhibited familiar form. Its classical shape is one which seems to many as something more traditional. When it was first built, however, this design was only just coming into use throughout the world, while earlier towers had consisted of as many as six or eight flattened sides.

Like many others, though, Cape Cod Light had a shape that was rounded to best withstand the winds and waters from whatever quadrant of the compass, and its base was widest to provide support. At the bottom of the tower, the brick walls are three feet thick, but hollow to provide insulation from the seasonal extremes of Cape Cod weather. The temperature inside was more critical for the proper maintaining of the oil than it was for the comfort of the keeper, who accepted the fact that he might be most busy when weather was at its worst; however, most towers were built with the keeper's access in mind.

"He led the way first through his

CUTTYHUNK LIGHT *no longer exists as a lighthouse. The site has been "hardened," and the beacon shines from atop a single steel tower. The island community itself, however, remains an outpost of Cape & Islands civilization. Much the same has happened at* DUMPLING ROCK, *not far across Buzzards Bay. Both lights had once helped guide New Bedford whalers safely home from voyages to the South Seas.*

79

bedroom, which was placed nearest to the light-house," wrote Thoreau of his climb to the top of the Cape Cod Light, "and then through a long, narrow, covered passage-way, between whitewashed walls like a prison entry into the lower part of the light-house, where many great butts of oil were arranged around; thence we ascended by a winding and open iron stairway, with a steadily increasing scent of oil and lamp-smoke to the trap door in an iron floor, and through this into the lantern.

"It was a neat building, with everything in apple-pie order, and no danger of anything rusting for want of oil," he said of the lantern room. "These were surrounded, at a distance of two to three feet, by large plate-glass windows, which defied the storms, with iron sashes, on which rested the iron cap. All the iron work, except the floor, was painted white. And thus the light-house was completed."

Outside the lantern room, a black-railed deck allowed the keeper to keep the panes as free from ice and dirt as

---

CUTTYHUNK
1823: Cuttyhunk Island, The Elizabeth Islands
STEEL FRAMEWORK STRUCTURE
Flashes white
RANGE: 12 MILES

Typical of many lighthouse stations throughout America, the lighthouse on Cuttyhunk no longer exists as a literal "lighthouse." Instead, the lantern which once sat atop the keeper's house has been replaced with a rather nondescript (and unromantic) framework structure of steel. While the remote island with its tiny village outpost remain a quaint destination for sailors and seasonal daytrippers, most lighthouse lovers generally find that traveling to Cuttyhunk for the sole purpose of viewing this site as it currently stands is not worth the required effort.

For passage to Cuttyhunk, see the *Transportation Appendix.*

he was possibly able. In Thoreau's day, that meant a winter wash with alcohol; today it is often undiluted Prestone to keep the ice from freezing. Always mindful of the inside temperature of the watch room to keep the oil sufficiently warm to readily burn, the keeper also had to keep the temperature of the lantern room cool enough to prevent any condensation or frost. And if the concern for too much moisture were not a constant worry, there was always the dust and pollen of the spring or the summertime problem of fluttering flocks of moths attracted by the light. Altogether, the glass surrounding the upper tower consisted of fourteen separate windows, each three panes high from lantern deck to ceiling.

LONG POINT LIGHT (below) *is still set atop a square, wooden tower; however, the keeper's house shown in this historic photo no longer exists. Though some might now think this shape is odd, a lighthouse with flat sides was typical before cast iron towers came into being.*

Today, the lowest level of glass has been replaced with solid panels.

Perhaps another seven feet below this deck outside the glass, a similar deck could be reached by iron ladder from the

one above or by a doorway from the watch room just beneath the lantern. Because the walls at that height are still a hefty eighteen inches thick, a double set of doors divides the inside from the out, much the way a bulkhead protects the holds within a ship. The inside set swings in, while the outer one often needs a push against the rushing wind. Once open, it faces the north-northwest to a view of Provincetown, the bay, and Plymouth far beyond. Behind the door, awaits the vast Atlantic, a greater sight than even Thoreau quite possibly imagined.

"Among the regulations of the Light-House Board, hanging against the wall here," observed Thoreau, "is one requiring the keeper to keep account of the number of

---

LONG POINT
1823: Provincetown
WHITE SQUARE TOWER
Fixed green
RANGE: 8 MILES

Like Provincetown's Wood End Light, this one is best seen from the water, but it can be seen with the naked eye from the town's MacMillan Wharf. Either private craft, or one of the several whale-watching vessels can provide an even better view.

Meanwhile, a properly documented off-road vehicle could get you closer. And the same could be said of a long trek through the sand. In short, neither can be reached without effort; however, here is one way to try.

Take Route 6 *all the way* to its end, where it intersects with Province Land Road. Take a right, then take your next left onto that part of Province Land Road which parallels Herring Cove Beach. If you can locate a safe and legal place to park your vehicle, then prepare yourself for a hike several miles to the south as you follow the curving shore. First you will encounter Wood End Light. If you still desire to hike to Long Point, keep in mind that you have walked only about a third of the overall distance you will need to cover on your roundtrip hike.

vessels which pass his light during the day. But there are a hundred vessels in sight at once, steering in all directions, many on the very verge of the horizon," he noted, "and he must have more eyes than Argus, and be a good deal farther sighted, to tell which are passing his light."

To be able to see those ships means they fall within the geographic range of Cape Cod Light; however, that does not assure that the beacon can be seen. A tower's height means nothing if the lamp is not clean or not bright enough. Engineers call this factor the *luminous range*, the distance at which the light actually is visible at sea. Even if its beam travels a straight line to the eye of the seaman, the luminous range can be disrupted by anything and everything from terrible weather conditions, to poor maintenance, to an inadequate source of light. While no keeper ever has control over conditions of the weather, he must constantly attend the light and make it shine the best it can. ✺

LONG POINT LIGHT *once displayed this original Cape Cod-style lighthouse, as did* CUTTYHUNK, MAYO BEACH, WING NECK, *and* NOBSKA. *Prior to the Civil War, this design was constructed along many parts of the young nation's shorelines. Because the heavy lantern was supported primarily by the ceiling beams, however, the entire apparatus often fell through the roof and crashed into the keeper's dwelling.*

CHAPTER 10
LESSONS SADLY LEARNED

IN ADDITION TO THE LIGHTHOUSE TOWER, a station might include other buildings: often an oil shed, sometimes a boathouse, and usually a dwelling of some sort. On occasion, however, the keeper found shelter within the tower itself. Perhaps the most poignant, as well as the most frightful of any episode involving such a structure involved the one which some have called the nation's most dangerous lighthouse, Minots Ledge, located offshore in the rocks just northwesterly from Cape Cod Bay.

Partially as a result of the Congressional investigation of 1838, a lighthouse was proposed for this general area, and almost ten years later a specific recommendation was made by the Topographical Department that an iron pile lighthouse be set upon Minots Rock. It was the best site off Cohasset, but it was still not an especially good site at all. For about three hours during low tide, an area only some twenty-five feet wide appeared above the water, and upon that Stephen Pleasonton would allow the construction of this relatively new style of tower. The prevailing thought was that the forces of water would meet with less resis-

EDGARTOWN HARBOR LIGHT now has a prefabricated cast iron tower that had marked the harbor in Ipswich, north of Boston. Aside from the fact that cast iron made for much easier construction, such towers also proved to be movable.

tance from a set of narrow iron piles than from any broader surface of stone.

The proposed design was this. Set in holes drilled five feet into the rock would be nine iron piles: eight of these

MINOTS LEDGE LIGHT, *patterned after lessons learned from the fabled* EDDYSTONE LIGHT, *also served as a model for* BISHOP & CLERKS, *southward of* POINT GAMMON *in Nantucket Sound.*

legs would be around the twenty-five foot perimeter, and the ninth would be in the center. Cemented into the rock, these eight legs would be braced around the outside, as well as to the ninth leg in the center. Atop them all would be placed the lantern; below that would be the keeper's quarters; and below them

BEACH POINT
1823: Sandy Neck, Barnstable
WHITE TOWER
Fixed white
RANGE: 11 MILES

No longer in commission, this light is private property among a colony of summer cottages at the eastern end of this barrier beach. It can be seen quite easily Blish Point in the village of Barnstable, and it can be reached by boat, as well as properly documented ORV.

To view it from shore, take Route 6 to Exit 6, then head north along Route 132 to the intersection with Route 6A. Take a right onto 6A, which is also the Main Street of Barnstable Village. Pass through the center of town to the traffic light, then turn left onto Mill Way. Stay on this road just about a mile until you come directly to the parking lot of Millway Beach. The abandoned tower of the lighthouse should be visible across the water and slightly to your right.

To reach the light by boat, you might ask for information at the nearby Millway Marina.

To reach the light by ORV, you must take Route 6A west and cross into the town of Sandwich. Just over the town line, Sandy Neck Road is on the right. Follow this to the information booth at the entrance to the beach, where there is a ranger on duty.

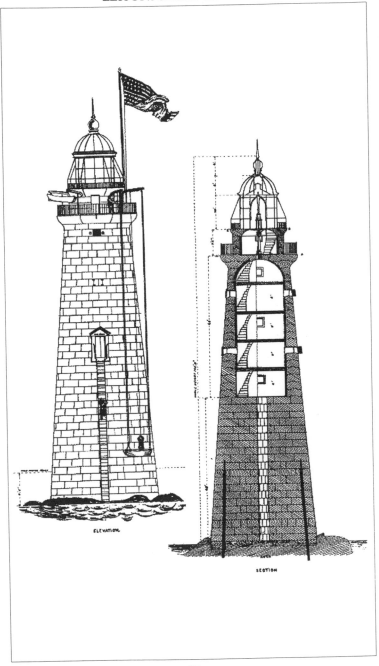

ELEVATION

SECTION

both, a supply deck nearly seventy feet above sea level. The project took nearly three years to finish, and when it was finally lighted on January 1, 1850, Minots Ledge tower was the first one in America fully exposed to the powers of the Atlantic Ocean.

By April of that year, Keeper Isaac Dunham and his assistants had experienced enough racking and straining at the mercy of the weather to implore the government to strengthen the tower; however, nothing was done, and Dunham resigned in October. The new keeper named was John Bennett, who not only suffered similar tossings as late into the following year as early April, but also forwarded similar complaints to the Fifth Auditor's office. An investigation was made, but the government did nothing more.

Then another storm blew across the Cape & Islands on April 16, 1851. When at last the fury subsided, the Minots Ledge Light was gone, reduced to twisted knot of iron stumps embedded in the ledge off Cohasset. With the lighthouse had perished the keeper's two assistants. Not too many months after that tragedy, gone as well would be the authority of the fifth auditor over the growing system of lighthouses. In 1852, a nine-member Lighthouse

EDGARTOWN HARBOR
1828: Edgartown, Martha's Vineyard
WHITE TOWER
Flashes red every 6 seconds
RANGE: 5 MILES

To visit this light, take Oak Bluffs Road into Edgartown, where the route of Main Street might vary with the season. For parking, you might do best by following the Main Street to its easternmost end, where there is public parking by Dock Street. Walk up Main Street, then take a right onto North Water Street. Less than a mile along, public access leads to the lighthouse itself.

For passage to the Vineyard, see the *Transportation Appendix*.

Board was created, and its authority matched its expertise. Among its earlier recommendations was the one which designated a more conventional stone tower for Minots Ledge. Thus, one of the system's worst mistakes was rectified with a most cogent decision.

EDGARTOWN HARBOR LIGHT originally had been built upon the end of riprap at the entrance to the harbor.

As with several area lighthouses of that period, such as BASS RIVER *in West Dennis, the original lantern was directly upon the roof of the keeper's dwelling.*

The new project took more than five years, from June of 1855 to August of 1860, and it patterned the tower after principles gleaned from England's famed Eddystone Light. The first forty feet of granite courses, dovetailed and interlocking, provided a solid foundation; the next forty feet was enough for a

storage space and a keeper's quarters, as well as the lantern house. A similar design would be applied in years to come at the lighthouse that sat on the ledge known as Bishop & Clerks, just offshore from West Yarmouth's Point Gammon in Nantucket Sound. Despite their structural innovations, however, these waterbound towers retained the conical shape which most identify still as being their idea of a lighthouse.

True, they might not have been the pure, white structures that most people have come to identify most readily with a lighthouse and its good intentions, but still they served their essential purpose. And even though the redstone tower at Gay Head, up-island on the Vineyard, has never glistened as a whitewashed daymark along the Cape & Islands shoreline, it nonetheless has always displayed a recognizable characteristic all its own. Still

DUMPLING ROCK
1828: Buzzards Bay, South Dartmouth
STEEL STRUCTURE
Flashes green
RANGE: 6 MILES

Like the lighthouse at Cuttyhunk, Dumpling Rock has been reduced to a steel structure. Though the site itself must have been an impressive one, the spartan pole (along with the fact that it can barely be viewed without a great deal of difficulty) makes any trip to the station rather uneventful.

If you feel you *must* go, take Route 6 west into Dartmouth, then turn left onto Slocum Road to South Dartmouth. Follow the signs into Padanaram. Cross the harbor bridge, then take your immediate left onto Smithneck Road. After a long, winding trip, you will come to Salters Point, clearly marked *private property*. Any further progress is an act of trespassing; however, a groundskeeper in the first building to the right might permit you a quick pass through to view what remains of the site at Dumpling Rock.

others, such as at Nauset Beach and Sankaty Head, were given identifiable bands of brilliant red.

In other instances, such as Wing Neck and Bass River Lights on the Cape, as well as the original lights at Cuttyhunk in the Elizabeths and at Edgartown Harbor on the Vineyard, the keeper's dwelling supported the lantern on its roof.

DUMPLING ROCK LIGHT resembled not only BIRD ISLAND, *just to its north, but also the stations of downeast Maine in that it sat fully upon a small, rockbound island of its very own. Most natural terrain surrounding the Cape & Islands is either sand or clay.*

Regardless, though, of whether a lighthouse looked like a whitewashed cone or a topless pyramid, whether a keeper's dwelling was made of wooden clapboard or roughened brick, the form was not of utmost importance, just as long as it stood up to nature. After all, what mattered most to the sailor at sea was not the house, but the light that it must support. ☀

CHAPTER 11
A LIGHT IN THE WINDOW

LIGHT HAS ALWAYS been invested by Mankind with powers much greater than its basic physical properties. The Greeks told stories not only of the Titan Prometheus, who first stole fire from the gods to benefit the mortals, but also of the virtuous Diogenes, who carried his lantern throughout the streets in search of an honest man. In countless civilizations across further generations since, the presence of light has come to symbolize the triumph of Knowledge over Ignorance, the triumph of Love over Hate, and essentially the triumph of Everything Good over Evil. Most still believe, after all, that it is better to light one small candle than to curse the darkness. In the case of a coastal lighthouse, truer thoughts were never held, for this particular pillar of fire came to symbolize the triumph of Safety over Danger, and the mere sighting of a lighthouse from land or from sea still can kindle a spark of emotion.

CAPE COD LIGHT, like GAY HEAD, now has four beams, each equal to four million candles, that come from thousand-watt bulbs behind these thirty-six inch lenses.

Throughout the entire history of these coastal lights, nearly every keeper has had to concern himself with a flame of one sort or another. In the earliest of times, the lights were little more than wood-burning fires upon the beach, or else baskets of coals hung on poles. Next came those fires set high up on hills; then wood fires placed atop towers. Aside from the fact that all this open flame allowed the actual rays of lights to escape aimlessly above and uncontrollably across the darkness of the night, these wood fires also required throughout the night a constant stoking by the keepers.

As nearby wood supplies around the lighthouse towers vanished when the trees were virtually depleted, first coal and then oil became the major sources of fuel for lighthouse lamps. Not only did coal provide a brighter, steadier glow which was more visible far at sea, but also it demanded less attention by the keeper. All too often, though, the keepers would abandon the coals for the evening, only to wake up and discover that their glowing heat had burned through their iron grates. In addition, coal and oil both produced a dimming soot that kept the

---

NOBSKA
1829: Woods Hole
WHITE TOWER
Flashes red every 6 seconds
RANGE: 16 MILES
An easy light to visit, this station sits atop the rocky headlands that overlook Vineyard Sound from the Cape.

Take Route 28 through Falmouth center and follow the signs to Woods Hole, which should lead you to Woods Hole Road. Follow this winding road nearly three miles to Church Street, on the left just before Coast Guard Station Woods Hole. If you see the buoy tenders tied to their docks off to your left — or else arrive at the Steamship Authority terminal — you've missed Church Street altogether.

Turn onto Church Street, which will lead you low along the rocky shore before the road dramatically rises and curves to the left. At the top of the rise is the lighthouse with limited parking allowed on the roadway.

keepers busy cleaning whatever glass surrounded the lantern.

Candles held some advantages, but even the invention of the electric light was slow in making its way into the lantern room. After all, most lighthouses

NOBSKA LIGHT once had this Cape Cod-style structure, complete with the saltbox roof and the air vent directed by a wind vane on its cap.

had been built so remotely distant from any sources of electrical power that a controllable flame remained the one type of lantern available. Only in the early 1930s, for example, did the Cape Cod Light change from its original source of light: oil-burning lamps.

When the station at Cape Cod was commissioned in

1797, the light was from a lantern room of spider lamps. These were little more than shallow pans of whale oil, each containing four solid, tubular wicks without any chimneys. Simple as these were, they caused a mess, because the spider lamps gave off a pungent smoke that not only soiled the lantern glass throughout the tower, but also prevented the keeper from staying very long within the lantern room to clean them.

Not long after the Cape Cod Light had been built, mariners began to report that they often had difficulty telling the difference between the Boston Light and this newer light to the south on Truro's High Lands. Only a few years earlier, the federal lighthouse legislation passed in 1792 had made it law that, "The light in the lighthouse shall be such as to distinguish it from others and prevent mistakes." So later, when a civil engineer reported to the government that there was "no way of telling one light from another on dark nights" and that there was "no accurate method of comparing intensity of one light to another, such as listing

NED POINT LIGHT is one of the easiest sites to visit and clearly displays a tower of whitewashed, rubblestone.

NED POINT
1837: Buzzards Bay, Mattapoisett
WHITE STONE TOWER
Flashes white
RANGE: 10 MILES
From the light at Bird Island, continue along Route 6 into Mattapoisett and take a left beyond the Police Station onto North Street. Follow North Street to the STOP sign at the bottom of the hill, where you will see the lighthouse off to your left across the water. Turn left onto Ned Point Road, which will lead you about 2 miles to a dirt parking lot that surrounds the lighthouse completely.

You might want to think about visiting the New Bedford lights from here.

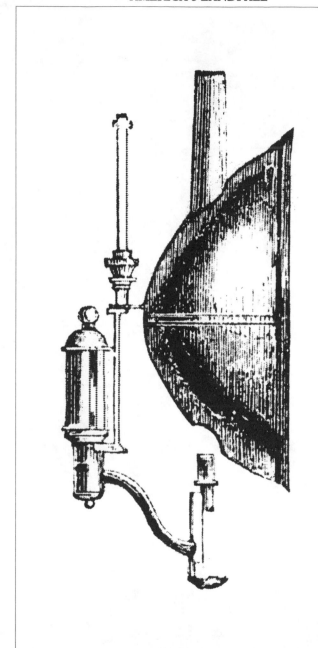

candlepower," Cape Cod Light was fitted with a mechanical eclipser in 1800.

Revolving slowly around the lantern, this consisted of a semi-circular screen which blocked out a portion of the light as it completed a rotation every eight minutes. The result at sea was the effect of a flashing beacon, the first in any American lighthouse. By 1807, however, the eclipser was removed after an inspector determined that too much of the light's intensity was being diminished. In short, the luminous range was being impaired for most of the time.

Meanwhile, within the next few years in England and in Europe, lighthouses were outfitted with a lamp invented by Aime Argand in 1781. Using a hollow tubular wick inside a glass chimney, the Argand lamp allowed oxygen not only to flow along both the inside and the outside of the wick, but also to burn with a brighter, smokeless flame that had the intensity of seven candles. When backed with a reflector shaped like a parabola, each Argand lamp could produce a light that was even four hundred times that brightness, the brightest lighthouse lanterns in the world. ⚝

CHATHAM LIGHT *now has revolving twin lights in its lone south tower. As at many other stations, the structure also serves as an collection station for weather data, as well as for radio transmissions.*

THE ARGAND LAMP *enabled the beam to shine with a brightness four hundred times greater than it had ever burned before.*

CHAPTER 12
AN IDEA NOT SO BRIGHT

UNFORTUNATELY, American ships were yet to see these Argand lamps shine from America's shores. Instead, Stephen Pleasonton's Wellfleet associate, Winslow Lewis, had developed in 1810 his own version of the Argand lamp and had sold the patent to the United States government just before the outbreak of the War of 1812. By 1815, all the lighthouses along the coast had a Lewis lamp. The lantern room at Cape Cod Light, for example, had fifteen new lamps arranged in two circular, horizontal rows. The outer, lower row held eight of the Lewis lamps, and the inner, upper row held seven; however, none of these was aimed due south across the lower Cape lands of Eastham and Chatham and Monomoy. Together with fifteen-inch reflectors, though, the fifteen new lamps were capable of sending out a brighter beam across the other three hundred degrees of the compass.

While the invention of Captain Lewis required only half the oil of the old spider lamps, his lamp was simply not as intense as the Argand lamp then being used in Europe. One reason was the early attempts by Lewis to increase each lamp's intensity by placing a lens

BISHOP & CLERKS LIGHT *marked rocks and shoals of Nantucket Sound just south of* POINT GAMMON. *As with* MINOTS LEDGE, *the tower could only be reached by an agile tender.*

in front of the flame. The idea made sense, because it was supposed to concentrate the straying beams of light; however, these lenses were removed before long, because they tended to block the beam instead.

The major reason, however, for the relative inferiority of the Lewis lamp was the shape of the so-called parabolic reflector. According to government reports, these tended to be less like reflecting mirrors and more like shaving basins. Their silver finish was too thin to withstand the daily cleaning, and their basic metal was unable to hold its parabolic shape. In fact, these reflectors were often reported to be more spherical than parabolic. By 1839, however, the Cape Cod Light had installed newer, twenty-one inch parabolic reflectors, and these were the ones that Thoreau had seen on his first visit to the tower on the High Lands.

"We walked slowly round in that narrow space as the keeper lighted each lamp in succession," he recalled, "conversing with him at the same moment that many a

---

MAYO BEACH
1838: Wellfleet
ONLY KEEPER'S HOUSE REMAINS
Fixed white
RANGE: 6 MILES

Like many of the local lights, the one at Mayo Beach has since been decommissioned (1922). In its various incarnations, the light has been a lantern atop the keeper's house, then an iron tower of various colors. Today, the site is only the keeper's house maintained as a private residence.

Take Route 6 to Wellfleet and turn onto the Main Street toward Wellfleet Center. Shortly after entering onto Main Street, you should take a left onto East Commercial Street. This colorful winding road leads you directly to the waterfront, where you should turn right at the harbor onto Beach Road. The former house of the keeper to of Mayo Beach Light is on your left, just beyond the beach parking lot.

sailor on the deep witnessed the lighting of the Highland Light. His duty was to fill and trim and light his lamps, and keep bright the reflectors. He filled them every morning, and trimmed them commonly once in the course of the night."

A lantern, however, was more than just a light. The principles behind its form were not unlike those of a handheld lantern; the scale was simply enlarged to the size of an entire room. Just above the keeper and his guest, a hole placed like the center of a funnel allowed the rising smoke and fumes to vent themselves into a flue between the ceiling and the cap. From there it could escape through trough-like gutters which then spilled down above the outside of the sashes. Just inside these sashes were a set of iron hooks on which a drape could hang across the plate glass windows of the lantern.

"This keeper noted that the centre of the beacon's flame

MAYO BEACH LIGHT *was tended for quite some time by Sarah Atwood. The site suffered constant erosion, and the repeated expenses of fill proved too costly to maintain the site. Today, only the Victorian-style keeper's dwelling remains.*

should be exactly opposite the centre of the reflectors," wrote Thoreau. "If he was not careful to turn down his wicks in the morning, the sun falling on the reflectors on the south side of the building would set fire to them, like a burning glass, in the coldest day, and he would look up at noon and see them all lighted! When your lamp is ready to give light, it is readiest to receive it, and the sun will light it."

Still, this was the work of the poorer reflectors and not of the best the world then knew. Technically, the concentrated beam produced by a parabolic reflector was the result of something called the catoptric system, and by 1820 the British were producing refined reflectors of silver-coated copper which made a single Argand lamp shine with the light of nearly 3,000 candles.

Not long after that, yet another technological advancement had been made in France when Augustin

---

WING NECK
1849: Bourne
WHITE TOWER
Fixed white
RANGE: 10 MILES
Now private property, the lighthouse should not be visited without asking permission. Though it is probably best seen these days from the waters of Buzzards Bay or Pocasset Harbor, the lighthouse can be reached by paved roadway.

Those with permission to visit should take Route 28 south from the Bourne Bridge rotary. Between Monument Beach and Pocasset, turn right onto Barlows Landing Road, which will take you for about three miles before crossing the railroad bed. Not far beyond that, Barlows Landing Road will continue to bear left, while Wing Neck Road will be the fork to the right. This continues a mile or so until it meets with Lighthouse Lane.

Again, this lighthouse is now a private residence, and any attempt to visit without permission is an act of trespassing.

Fresnel produced a lens that used the dioptric system. While the catoptric system of the parabolic reflector bounced the light into a stronger beam, the dioptric system of the Fresnel lens used a set of prisms to collect and bend and aim whatever light came from an Argand lamp. Eventually, these lenses and the light they produced would be categorized into orders, each determined by the distance from the light source itself to the glass of the lens.

WING NECK LIGHT *overlooks Buzzards Bay from the western coast of Cape Cod. This photo shows several structural elements common among lighthouse stations, including the covered passageway between the keeper's house and the light tower, as well as the pyramid shaped building that supported the bell used as a fog signal.*

A so-called *first order* lens was both the largest and the brightest of the four most common sizes, and it measured 36.2 inches from light source to lens glass. A lens of the *second order* was 27.6 inches; of the *third order*, 19.7 inches; and the *fourth*, 9.8. The first two orders were used for seacoast lights; the others, more commonly for harbor and range lights.

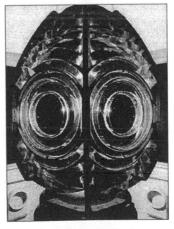

The basic result of Fresnel's invention was the creation of the most efficient lantern yet, not

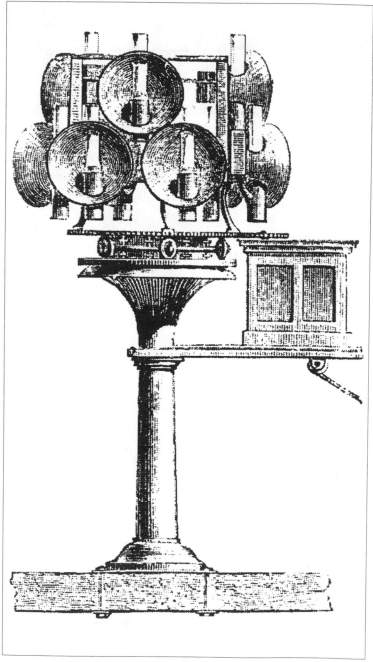

simply one which lost no light beams to the ceiling or the floor, to the heavens or the ocean, but also one which saved more ships out on the seas. Using a single Argand lamp, the Fresnel lens could create a beam as bright as 80,000 candles, the equivalent of today's automobile headlight. With the Fresnel lens, moreover, that beam of light could be shone directly where the sailors needed it most. ☀

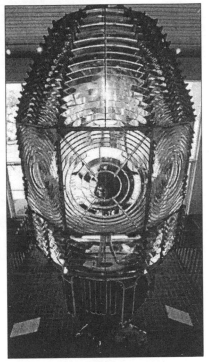

FRESNEL LENS *of the first order, such as those at* CAPE COD, SANKATY HEAD, *and* GAY HEAD *were large enough for an adult to stand within the glass itself.*

CHATHAM'S *lens (page 105) is on display outside the Chatham Historical Society.*

CATOPTRIC APPARATUS *enabled Argand lamps mounted upon a pedestal to rotate by means of cogs, wheels, and chains. As each lamp entered a seaman's line of vision, the light appeared to flash. An improvement over the eclipser, this apparatus never dimmed or obscured the light.*

CHAPTER 13
BEYOND A BETTER BEAM

DUE TO THE CLOSE RELATIONSHIP between Lewis and Pleasonton the Fresnel lens was slow in reaching the shores of the North America. For all the changes being made in shipbuilding and ship propulsion, as well as all the changes coming about in lighthouse tower construction, the light source itself remained less than its brightest. In the years before the Civil War, the United States government had purchased three of these Fresnel lenses for experimentation, and one was placed out at Sankaty Head on Nantucket in 1851.

Meanwhile, the Lewis lamp continued to find friends in high places, and the installation of the Argand lamp would never take place on the coast of Cape Cod. Instead, the lighthouse would be equipped with yet another type of lamp which would better deliver the fuel directly to the flame. This was a blessing for the keeper, because the use of the Fresnel lens also meant the need for fewer lamps. The fifteen Lewis lamps in Cape Cod Light, for example, were replaced with a single, four-wick hydraulic lamp. With these improvements, though, came a complicated set of cogs

EAST CHOP LIGHT *now sports a coat of classic white after having also been painted shades of gray and brown. In earlier days, this same site had served as a semaphore station that exchanged flag signals across the Vineyard Sound with one at Nobska Point.*

and springs and pumps which baffled any keeper who had lacked the necessary mechanical inclination.

These particular lamps would also be among the last to burn whale oil being brought back to these shores in dwindling quantities by the fleets from Nantucket and New Bedford. By 1860, Cape Cod Light would be relying upon lard oil and eventually kerosene. That final switch in the 1880s to an oil refined, rather than one rendered, would help reduce any worry about cold temperatures pervading the tower and congealing animal oils into lumps of fat. At the time of the installation of the hydraulic lamps, though, the winter oil remained a problem, ao did the lamps themselves.

These hydraulic lamps, after all, represented the first real pieces of machinery in a lighthouse. Fog bells and steam whistles were sometimes employing clockworks and large engines, but these lamps were more complicated

---

PAMET HARBOR
1849: Truro
LANTERN ON KEEPER'S QUARTERS
Fixed red
RANGE: 6 MILES

Though the lighthouse no longer exists at this site, the Pamet remains one of the most colorful sites in Cape & Islands lore. With headwaters in the wetlands just behind the fragile Ballston Beach on the east coast of the Cape, the Pamet River flows west until it empties into Pamet Harbor and Cape Cod Bay. At one time, the site was among the five considered for the dredging of a canal through the Cape; however, any shortcut from the bay through to the Atlantic would still not spare the ships from the dangerous shoals just beyond the Great Outer Beach. The other sites included: Jeremiah's Gutter from Rock Harbor to Town Cove in Orleans; Bass River to Cape Cod Bay between Dennis and Yarmouth; Hyannis Harbor to Barnstable Harbor; and the existing site of the Cape Cod Canal.

gadgets. Their function was to keep the level of the oil inside the wick just below the very burning of the flame, and they seemed both intricate and delicate. In the event there was any problem or question with these new contraptions, the keeper need only read the instructions. But all too often a keeper's qualifications might not have included that

CHATHAM'S TWIN LIGHTS *were the last built on the site before the government removed the north (right) tower to Eastham, as the single* NAUSET *replacing the legendary "Three Sisters."*

skill and generally there was no one else around; experience soon became a teacher at the risk of wrecking a ship on the shore.

If the hydraulic lamps presented an occasional drawback, though, then at least the Fresnel lens provided for a steady performance. More than either the catoptric system, or even the original di-optric system, today's Fresnel lens is called a *catadioptric* system, because it contains elements of both. Each lens panel in this particular system consists of a central bull's-eye lens to concentrate the rays coming horizontally from the lamp. Above and below each panel,

SOUTH HYANNIS LIGHT *once guided passenger and cargo vessels through Lewis Bay, then on into the Hyannis inner harbor. Most of this shipping traffic was to and from Nantucket.*

sits a series of glass prisms; the lower ones refract light up to the beam from the bull's -eye lens, while the upper rings

refract the light down to it. This results in a single,

SOUTH HYANNIS LIGHT *was built as a range light by Daniel Snow Hallett to align with* HYANNIS *at the head of the harbor.*

concentrated beam more intense than any other to date.

Most often in lighthouses, these panels are a cone-shaped lens resembling a bee-hive nearly twelve feet

SOUTH HYANNIS
1849: Hyannis Port
WHITE RUBBLESTONE CONE
Fixed white
RANGE: 8 MILES

As with the lighthouse at Wings Neck, this is now a private residence and should not be visited without permission; however, the squat white cone can be seen from either the beach, or from the harbor.

To get to Sea Street Beach, take Route 6 to Exit 6 and follow Route 132 about four miles to the traffic rotary. After entering into the rotary traffic, you should take your second right onto Barnstable Road. Take Barnstable Road straight for a little more than a mile to Main Street.

At Main Street, turn right and plan to move into the left lane of this one-way street. Nearly another mile along Main Street, you'll come to the third set of traffic lights. This is Sea Street. Turn left, cross South Street, and follow Sea Street to where it bears right and becomes Ocean Avenue. Bear right and you will see the parking lot for Sea Street Beach.

On Sea Street Beach you will see to the east a breakwater, from which you will find a clear view of the private residence that once was South Hyannis Light.

To view the lighthouse from an outbound vessel in Hyannis Harbor, watch over the starboard for the breakwater that marks the end of Kalmus Park Beach. From the southern end of that breakwater, look westward to the long breakwater that extends southeast from Hyannis Port. The lighthouse site is nearly mid-way between those two breakwaters.

For commercial passage through Hyannis Harbor, see the *Transportation Appendix.*

tall. Then, if the Fresnel lens is rotated, the moving set of bull's-eye lenses present the effect of a flashing beacon. Unlike the eclipser, this beacon never loses its luminous range; it only grows in intensity as the bull's-eye passes between the lamp in the tower and the observer at sea.

The Fresnel lens installed in Cape Cod Light was not the catadioptric system, but rather the original dioptric system. Lacking the bull's-eye lens in

MINOTS LEDGE LIGHT *remains a legend in the annals of the U.S. Lighthouse Service, as well as a controversial symbol of the system's tenacity and dedication to saving lives.*

the middle panel, the lens instead was rectangular, but still a vast improvement over the Lewis version of the Argand lamp. This light would remain about the same until the turn of the century, when once again the

MINOTS LEDGE
1850: Cohasset
GRAY GRANITE CONE IN THE WATER
Flashes white 1-4-3 each 30 seconds
RANGE: 15 MILES

Because you can easily plan to view this light within minutes of seeing The Gurnet and Scituate Light to the south, the directions to Minots Ledge begin with directions to the Gurnet, then continue with directions from Scituate. The arrow on the thumbnail map is not misplaced; it indicates the approximate site of Cohasset in relation to the other landmarks.

Coming from Scituate Light, turn right at the traffic light onto Beaver Dam Road. Pass through another set of lights, then come to yet one more. Turn right onto Country Way.

At the fork where Country Way curves to continue left, bear right at Hollet Street and follow this to the end. Turn right onto Henry Turner Bailey Road, where you will quickly come to a small parking lot at Minots Beach. From there, you can see the lighthouse off to your left in the water.

To return to Route 3A, simply follow back along Henry Turner Bailey Road, where it will eventually end at Route 3A.

government decided that the Cape Cod Light should flash.

By October of 1901, the lamp — which stood twelve feet tall and reached some six feet in diameter — was sitting upon a chariot and floating on a frictionless pool of liquid mercury that allowed the lamp to revolve with the least amount of effort. Straight down through the deck of the lantern room to the watch room right below hung a massive clockwork system to rotate the heavy lamp. Though cumbersome, the clockwork was not intricate.

Basically, it consisted of a large steel drum, around which was wrapped a weighted cord. By engaging a clutch, the keeper could turn a hand crank to wind the cord around the drum without moving the lamp. Then, as gravity pulled the weight on the end of the cord straight down through the lantern room deck, the drum would turn and a set of gears would mesh with the cog wheel at the base of the lens chariot and rotate the Cape Cod Light. As it flashed once every four seconds, mariners needed only to refer to their light list to know which government lighthouse stood there within their sight.

With the adding of the flashing signal at the High Lands came other 20th-century advancements which would begin to transform the basic function of the lighthouse out in Truro and along the coastline of the United States. By 1904, the government had established a United States Naval Radio Station on the lighthouse grounds and this, in turn, became a radio compass station. With the rapid development of the radio compass and the radio beacon, both would replace in time the need for most ships to visibly locate any light upon the Cape & Islands' shores. This, in fact, has become the fate of most of the lights throughout the nation. While each lighthouse remains more than merely decorative, its visible beam stands to serve the less sophisticated sailors.

That has not meant the end of continued improved conditions in the Cape & Islands lighthouses. Although an electric light was slow to come to the High Lands tower,

come it did in 1931 when the last of the oil lamps was replaced with a 1,000-watt bulb inside the Fresnel lens. Actually, more than one was first placed inside on a starfish-looking mechanism which rotated automatically to a newer, working bulb whenever one burns out.

ELECTRIC LIGHTS *now beam out from* CAPE COD *across the Great Outer Beach and the North Atlantic.*

Finally, in 1945 the Fresnel lens was dismantled and scrapped to make way for two pair of rotating beacons which together send out four beams of four million candlepower each. Shaped more like drums, the lamps have a thirty-six inch lens on each end and are set one on top of the other so that the lamps are 180 degrees apart. The lenses now are circular, more like those in an airport tower, and behind each shines a 1,000-watt bulb. It is paired with another bulb all set to rotate into place when the first bulb does burn out. An electric motor drives the mechanism that continues to rotate the four beacons at the same rate of one flash every four seconds. Gone is the fabled flame, and with it the legendary keeper.

And yet, the keeper's legacy endures. ⚡

Chapter 14
LEGACY OF THE KEEPER

FIRST, THERE WERE THE KEEPER'S DUTIES, sometimes arduous, but seldom intellectual. Early generations of keepers tending spider lamps often needed only to fill the pans with oil, light the wicks, and clean the panes of glass quite often; later generations tending to the Lewis version of the Argand lamp, had to trim the wicks, clean the chimneys, and avoid doing whatever possibly might scratch the parabolic reflectors. For this, they came to be known affectionately as "wickies," and as long as the keeper was attentive each night, was fully prepared for the following night by the middle of each morning, and was tidy enough to apply to his cleaning the minimal efforts of a "Scotch lick," then the primary routine required little more than stamina and common sense.

But "keep" is a word that deserves more thought than most folks tend to give it. As innocent as it may look at first, the syllable resounds with trust, as well as obligation. Consider, for example, what a person did to lay claims to being a keeper. In general, one must: keep alert, keep watch, keep calm, keep clean, keep accounts, keep at hand, keep house, keep track of time, and always try to keep healthy. All this was done to

CLEVELAND LEDGE LIGHT *rests upon an iron caisson buried in Buzzards Bay. This was the very last lighthouse ever commissioned in New England; after this followed the so-called "Texas towers."*

119

keep a ship away from harm. After all, in keeping to themselves they had become dedicated keepers of faith, the faith that bonded keepers and captains together through the dangers of the darkness.

"It requires a lot of philosophy to be a light-keeper on an outside station," remarked the late Captain Charles Hinckley, who had served five miles south of Cape Cod in the lighthouse that marked rocks known as Bishop & Clerks. Built in 1858, the granite tower was damaged by a storm in 1935, then demolished by the Coast Guard in 1952. Much like the structure at Minots Ledge, the tower at Bishop & Clerks emerged straight up from a ledge beneath the waters, so it served both as a dwelling and a light. "The trouble with our life here," remarked a keeper at Minots Ledge, "is that we have too much time to think."

PALMER ISLAND LIGHT *was the first to have its tower illuminated on the outside so that the beacon above could be distinguished even more readily from the competing lights in the skyline of New Bedford seen behind it by vessels at sea.*

PALMER ISLAND
1851: New Bedford Harbor
WHITE TOWER
Flashes white
RANGE: 8 MILES

Since the construction of the hurricane lock at the mouth of the Acushnet River, the abandoned lighthouse now stands within the protected confines of the stone dike between Fairhaven and New Bedford. Because the New Bedford fishery separates the site from the busy roadway known as Rodney French, both public safety and private property make this a difficult lighthouse to visit. You might plan to be satsified with a distant view.

As you follow Route 6 from Mattapoisett to New Bedford, plan to slow at the bridge across the Acushnet River so that you can gaze at the lighthouse along the right shore just beyond the fishing fleet and the fish processing plants.

That did not mean that there were an extraordinary number of idle hours in a keeper's day. On the contrary, there were many duties, most of which were mindless chores that could be handled while contemplating other matters. Aside from tending to the lantern at regular intervals throughout the hours of darkness, a keeper then had to refill the lamps and trim the wicks by 10:00 the next morning in preparation for the coming night. In addition, the brass and glass of the lantern room and tower required

SANKATY HEAD LIGHT *had a Fresnel lens of the first order that is shown in this archival photograph. As was characteristic of most images from this period, the keeper and members of his family posed at their stations. On the lantern deck here, they serve as a measure of the immense size of this lens.*

SANKATY HEAD
1850: Siasconset, Nantucket
WHITE TOWER WITH RED BAND
Flashes white every 4.5 seconds
RANGE: 24 MILES

To approach Sankaty Head on land from Nantucket town, travel easterly on Orange Street to the rotary at Milestone Road, then take the Milestone Road east to the village of Siasconset. Just past the water pump at the center of the village, turn left onto Sankaty Avenue. About a mile along this road you will come to the lighthouse.

For a little more dramatic approach to the site, you might want to make this a longer drive from the Polpis Road direction, where you will first encounter the site of the tower across the legendary moors of Nantucket. If so, after you first come to the rotary at Milestone Road, take Milestone Road less than a half mile, then bear left onto Polpis Road. Continue on Polpis Road about four miles to where it intersects with Quidnet Road. Quidnet Road continues almost straight ahead, while Polpis Road goes to your right, where it eventually becomes Sankaty Avenue. Soon you'll see the banded tower of Sankaty Head Light ahead and to the left of the road.

For passage to Nantucket island, see the *Transportation Appendix.*

constant cleaning and polishing, as well as occasional replacement and repair. Beyond the tower itself, the entire station demanded the sort of constant attention that ranged from ordinary housekeeping and maintenance to bookkeeping and management.

Always there were other tasks. If a station had a boat-shed and a landing, then a high wind or a heavy sea might inflict some damage needing his attention. Inside and out, the tower needed constant care: the spiral staircase needed painting, as did the lantern's decks; walls had to be kept free of cracks, whose presence not only weakened the tower against the winds, but also made for cold conditions that threatened to thicken the oil; and always panes of glass had to be replaced. Sands driven by the winds would etch the surface and diminish the light,

---

BASS RIVER
1855: West Dennis
LANTERN ON KEEPER'S HOUSE
Flashes white every 6 seconds
RANGE: 12 MILES
Now expanded into The Lighthouse Inn, which has been owned and operated by the Stone Family for more than half a century, the keeper's quarters on West Dennis Beach still support the lantern that was recommissioned in 1989 as a seasonal aid to navigation.

Take Route 6 to Exit 9, where you should take Route 134 south. Follow this road to its *very* end. To do this, you will need to know that Route 134 eventually intersects with Route 28. Upon crossing Route 28, the roadway becomes Swan Pond River Road, a winding road in the town of Dennis. After two miles, this road will end altogether at Lower County Road.

Turn right onto Lower County Road and travel about a half mile until the road begins to bear right into School Street; on your left, you should expect to see Lighthouse Road and signs to The Lighthouse Inn. Turn left and you will come to the inn another half mile down the road.

and now and then a bird or two would
smash against the lantern panes. To
neglect any single one of these most
commonplace occurrences would be to
invite a trouble. A conscientious keeper
understood that responsibility.

That is why from the earliest of
available openings at lighthouse stations, the job of keeper seemed most

BASS RIVER LIGHT
*had guided mariners across
the shoals of Nantucket
Sound, where the keeper's
dwelling with its rooftop
lantern rested not more
than a mile east of the
mouth of Bass River. The
station now serves as the
hospitable Lighthouse Inn.*

fitting for any one of a number of folks whose interests
already had taken them to sea. "We know how eyes may
be strained in thick weather at sea to get hold of the
light," explained one such gent, "and that makes us
painfully anxious to keep it up to its full power, especially
when frosts or sea-scud dims the lantern; for that is the
very time when minutes count for hours on board ship."

Still, not every lighthouse station was set on some edge of the mainland, where a keeper might maintain a homestead in town; more than a few — such as Bishop & Clerks, Minots Ledge, Butler Flats, Duxbury Pier (Bug), and later Cleveland Ledge — became outposts of civilization that were set astride a sometimes savage sea. If a keeper were fortunate, then he might have either an assistant, or his family to help. Quite commonly, his appointed assistant was his wife, who could reside there, more often than not, with their children. As a result, an offspring's upbringing would be centered around both the sea and the tasks that were always at hand. Raised in such surroundings, certain sons and daughters knew nothing more than what it was to be a keeper; some even knew what that meant, for that became their second nature. Nevertheless, by the end of the 19th century, every such wife and offspring of a lighthouse keeper who might aspire to rise to a similar position in life would have to meet the keeper's qualifications set forth by the Lighthouse Board.

CLEVELAND LEDGE LIGHT, *as well as* BUTLER FLATS *and* DUXBURY PIER (Bug) *each rested upon iron caissons embedded into the bottom of their respective waters. To accomplish this, workers followed a shaft to a bottom airlock, where they dug into the sand and silt. Debris was removed through the same shaft, then workers left. The iron tube was filled with concrete.*

BISHOP & CLERKS
1858: South of Point Gammon, Nantucket Sound
GRANITE TOWER
Flashed white
RANGE: 13 MILES

No longer standing, the site of the station is now marked as a navigational hazard, and it is visible from the port rail of any vessel departing Hyannis Harbor.

For passage through the harbor, see the *Transportation Appendix*.

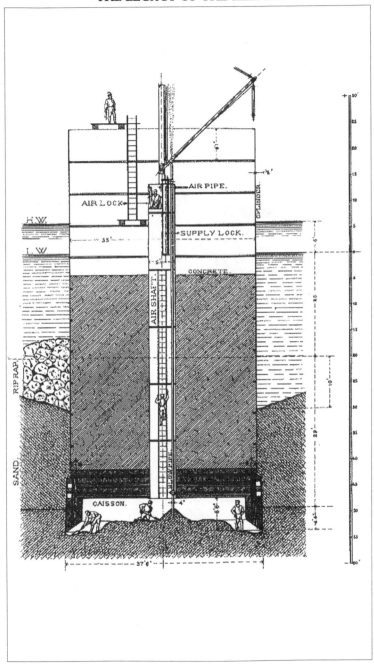

In an effort to reduce patronage in the system, the board restricted appointees to those between eighteen and fifty who not only could read, write, and maintain a ledger, but also could master the skills and rigors of a lighthouse station. Sometimes that entailed carpentry; other times, mechanics; and on some occasions, dangerous rescues.

What a keeper did not know, he — and, sometimes, *she* — was

SPIRAL STAIRWAY
of Cape Cod Light is seen from beneath as it winds upward to the oil deck (semi-circle in the center of this photo), just below the lantern deck. From this vantage point, the bottoms of the cast-iron steps are twisting up to the left, where they stop at a landing that is about a ¼ turn of the tower's inside circumference and is braced by black iron beams to the brick wall.

expected to be able to find in the station's collection of reference manuals that explained almost everything from lens cleaning to lantern repair to machinery operations. For recreational reading, there was also a more casual collection of about forty books kept in a portable bookshelf at every station. Every three months or so, these would be taken to another lighthouse by the station tender which brought provisions and replaced this library with another collection. All this was the system's concept of doing battle with a keeper's desolation.

Though some outside station sites even offered keepers and their families just a little more space than those at Bishop & Clerks might have suffered, almost every keeper was a man of devotion; so much so that such devotion to the light would become the touchstone of many careers in the lighthouse service, even after the Lighthouse Board was formally dissolved by Congress in 1910 and replaced by a civilian Bureau of Lighthouses at the same time.

Clearly, the old organization relinquished a more reputable lighthouse system than the one it had inherited from the Superintendency of the Fifth Auditor. And before administration of the system would next be given over to the Coast Guard in 1939, even greater changes would come about. None of these calculated improvements, however, could ever overshadow the poignant dedication of its emerging breed of keepers and their families. ☀

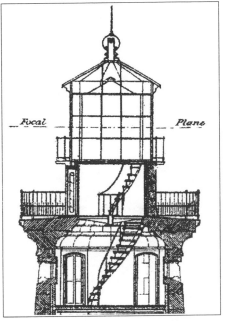

THE LANTERN ROOM *in this cutaway is between the spiral staircase (from deck to deck below) and the ball-shaped vent cap with the lightning rod above.*

DUXBURY PIER LIGHT, *with its rockbound caisson exposed, appears to be higher only because of an astronomical low tide. Note the tender suspended from the lantern deck.*

129

CHAPTER 15
AS DAY FOLLOWS NIGHT

ON ANY GIVEN MORNING along these Cape & Islands shores, the signs still do appear of what has always seemed a waking, timeless life: the stars all yield their hopeful gleams to the rays of a brilliant sun; the shorebirds lift their restless wings to the rise of a stiffening breeze; and the sands and stones all cleanse themselves in the wash of a briny wave. A glorious end to a peaceful night, this kind of morning was long the dream of keepers and captains alike, but the men on the lantern galleries and the men on their quarterdecks all knew that dreams were never meant to last forever. As well, they understood that dreams were never, ever at all the things they might appear; on occasion, a dream might even mask a nightmare. So much for beauty. Reality was the reason why men first built their lighthouses on this land they called Cape Cod and the Islands, the nearest edge of an endless sea whose hidden dangers seemed eternal.

Even though some things never seemed to change, countless others did. By the end of the 19th century, for example, the eastern seaboard no longer remained a frontier, but had become instead a gateway to inland wonders. America was headed west. Some moved by prairie

DUXBURY PIER LIGHT *is one of many throughout the world often called "bug" lights because of their towers' bug-like appearance in the water from a distance.*

schooner; others, by iron horse; and more than a few, by boats that steamed along rivers and even man-made canals. This was the nation's progress, rooted deeply in earlier travels upon the ocean, where none could ever anticipate any such thing they might call an airship.

Still, these Cape & Islands lighthouses remained important to its people, not only as a recognition of the shoreline's constant hazards, but also as an expression of the kinship that bound together throughout those less hospitable nights one stranger on the shore with countless others at sea. After all, if men could not change the dangers at hand, then at least they might face them together.

After the start of the 20th century, greater changes meant fewer ones for the Cape & Islands shores. Less than a dozen new lighthouse stations would ever be added to all of this New England coastline that had held them first. This slackened pace in the posting of this treacherous shoreline reflected two undeniable truths: one was that these waters had become rather well-marked; the other, that newer ports and waterways throughout the growing nation were demanding as much attention.

Still, there were other reasons. By 1914, for example,

DUXBURY PIER (BUG)
1871: Duxbury Harbor
WHITE IRON TOWER ON CAISSON
Fixed red
RANGE: 3 MILES

Squatting in the water, the Bug marks the channel just west of the Gurnet. You can view it from Plymouth's waterfront, or approach it by boat.

From the Sagamore Bridge, take Route 3 north to Route 44 into Plymouth Center.

For passage through the harbor at Plymouth, see the *Transportation Appendix*.

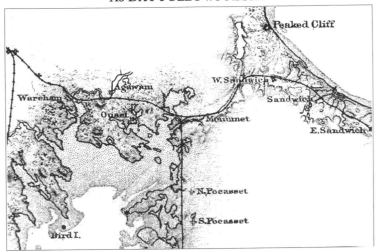

the Cape Cod Canal was completed to connect the waters of Cape Cod Bay with those of Buzzards Bay, just to the west of the peninsula. Basically the excavation across the Cape Cod mainland of an almost natural waterway created by the Scusset and Manomet Rivers, this canal had been envisioned as early as 1627 when Governor Bradford first established a trading post with the Dutch along those same two brackish creeks. Later, the British had foreseen a similar advantage during the Revolutionary War, and so had President Washington thereafter.

CAPE COD CANAL *was still a mariner's dream on this 19th-century chart. The railroad tracks follow the Manomet and Scusset Rivers from Buzzards Bay to Cape Cod Bay. The black dots mark the lights at* BIRD ISLAND *and* WING NECK.

When the Cape Cod Canal was finally realized in the 20th century, then, a good many prudent ship captains found reason to avoid the slower and shallower route of old that had taken their vessels through both the Vineyard and Nantucket Sounds, then around to the treacherous outer side of this angled, sandy peninsula. The canal saved time, but it also saved ships and lives.

In addition to that engineering feat, the 20th century was proving to be a period of extraordinary change. For one thing, other American ports, such as New York, had emerged, rivaled, and in many ways surpassed the older ports throughout Cape Cod, Nantucket & Martha's Vineyard. For another, there were developed newer modes of moving both cargo and passengers. In addition, there were related improvements in ways to navigate the waters of the world.

Along with better ways to illuminate a lighthouse lantern came progress with those invisible radio waves. After the end of World War II, radar was in widespread use. Not long after that followed LORAN, and now global positioning systems (GPS), each of which — in conjunction with the use of radar — has all but eliminated the likelihood that the master of any sophisticated vessel might ever need to witness with his eyes those dangers

WOOD END
1872: Provincetown
WHITE SQUARE TOWER
Flashes red every 10 seconds
RANGE: 13 MILES

Like Provincetown's Long Point Light, this one is best seen from the water, but it can be seen with the naked eye from the town's MacMillan Wharf. Either private craft, or one of the several whale-watching vessels would provide an even better view.

Meanwhile, a properly documented off-road vehicle could get you closer. And the same could be said of a long trek through the sand. In short, neither can be reached without effort; however, here is one way to try.

Take Route 6 *all the way* to its end, where it intersects with Province Land Road. Take a right, then take your next left onto that part of Province Land Road which parallels Herring Cove Beach. If you can locate a safe and legal place to park your vehicle, then prepare yourself for a hike several miles to the south as you follow the curving shore. First you will encounter Wood End Light. If you still desire to hike to Long Point, keep in mind that you have walked only about a third of the overall distance you will need to cover on your roundtrip hike.

waiting ahead. To such seamen, the light-house had become little more than an orna-ment, a reflection of beauty and light. To the skipper of a smaller craft, however, the sight of a lighthouse still held a noble pur-pose. As late as the end of the 20th century, small boaters continue to believe as much.

WOOD END LIGHT *no longer is surrounded by all the outbuildings shown in this archival photograph; however, it still retains its four-sided tower.*

With the sturdy reconstruction of the original lights, along with this shrinking need for any more, the construc-tion of lighthouses along this shoreline came to a glorious halt. The last commissioned in all of New England was the stylistic tower of Cleveland Ledge Lighthouse in Buzzards Bay, not far from the western entrance to the Cape Cod Canal. Commissioned in 1943, its unique motif is unchurac-teristic of any frugal, Yankee heritage, and it closely resembles instead the art deco lines of some other time and place. ☀

CHAPTER 16
TRIMMING THE LIGHTS

WHILE CLEVELAND LEDGE WAS THE LAST of the originals to be built anywhere in New England, several others were being either decommissioned, or automated by the Coast Guard throughout the Cape & Islands. A new style of light was constructed in 1951 as a platform to replace the lightship at Buzzards Bay, but at places such as Stage Harbor Light in Chatham and Beach Point Light on Sandy Neck, the lanterns have been removed and the dwellings have been purchased for use to this day as private homes. At places like Monomoy Island Light south of the Cape, the abandoned stations that once had fallen into states of unsightly disrepair have since been restored by private foundations which still recognize the heritage that rightly belongs to America's lights.

Meanwhile, still other lighthouses have remained lighted by private owners, such as the Bass River Light in West Dennis, which has been operated as The Lighthouse Inn for more than a half century by the Stone family.

The concern and care for the restoration of abandoned lighthouses has fallen not only under the jurisdiction of several state and local historical commissions, but also within the specific concern of several private

STAGE HARBOR LIGHT *is now a private residence whose romantic setting still attracts the attention of beachcombers who stroll Nantucket Sound.*

groups, such as Save Cape Cod Light in Truro, the Nauset Light Preservation Society in Eastham, and the Friends of Sankaty Head on Nantucket, while others share a concern for those lighthouses which fall within the scope of a much broader orientation, such as the Lighthouse Preservation Society based in Rockport, Massachusetts, and the New England Lighthouse Preservation Society in Wells, Maine. In addition, they work in harmony with agencies of the Federal government, such as the National Park Service and the United States Coast Guard, as well as state, county, and local authorities. Regardless of their individual scopes, the aim of such groups remains undeniably true, and that is to restore and preserve the lighthouses throughout Cape Cod, Nantucket & Martha's Vineyard.

EAST CHOP LIGHT *allows a close-up example of the seams between each prefabricated section of cast iron, as well as of the Victorian-era windows.*

As an altogether distinct project, though, the reconstruction of the

EAST CHOP
1872: Oak Bluffs, Martha's Vineyard
WHITE TOWER
Flashes green every 6 seconds
RANGE: 9 MILES

This lighthouse is closer and much simpler to reach from Oak Bluffs, where the ferry service is only seasonal. Because of space limitations, however, these are the longer directions for the year-round service from Vineyard Haven.

From Main Street, turn left and follow Beach Road past the petroleum tanks and over the bridge at Lagoon Pond. Just over the bridge, Beach Road will turn right into Eastville Avenue. Keep to the left and follow the road along the shoreline. At Highland Drive, bear left and follow the road between the harbor and Crystal Lake. As it curves uphill and to the right, you will come directly to the lighthouse.

For passage to the Vineyard, see the *Transportation Appendix.*

Great Point Light on Nantucket remains in a class by itself. Though the first wooden tower had been built in 1784, it was replaced with a rubblestone tower in 1816 after the original had burned to the sands the year before. Then, in 1984, the second tower was reduced to a heap in the midst of a spring nor'easter.

Given the state of 20th-century engineering and technology, any one of a number of structures easily could have been adapted and built to replace the faraway island's northernmost lighthouse; however, the people of Nantucket clearly wished that the new one retain its island heritage, so the United States Coast Guard commissioned the architectural and engineering firm of Ganteaume & McMullen in Boston to replicate the original Great Point Light. The mandate was nothing less than unique; the challenge, intriguing.

STAGE HARBOR
1880: Chatham
WHITE TOWER
Fixed white
RANGE: 12 MILES

With the lantern no longer atop the tower and the station decommissioned, the lighthouse is now a private residence. As such, it should not be visited without permission from the owner. Any attempt to do so can be considered an act of trespassing. Still, a fine view of the station can be found with a trek along Hardings Beach.

Take Route 6 to Exit 11, then follow Route 137 south to Route 28. At Route 28, turn left and pass through the village of West Chatham. Just beyond the village, turn right onto Barn Hill Road and follow it to the fork with Hardings Beach Road, where you should bear right. Once you come to the parking lot, try to find a space as far to the distant end as possible, because there is still a good little hike ahead along the beach.

Follow the shore to the east, where the private residence that was once a lighthouse stands at the entrance to Stage Harbor.

More than just a reproduction, the new structure took advantage of some opportunities to include engineering improvements. While the visual design is based indeed upon earlier drawings, salvaged pieces, and related historical information, its technological and structural design are based upon the most recent military specifications. The shaft of the tower is concrete coated with acrylic; the electric lighting is powered by batteries

recharged with solar panels; and the cofferdam foundation is buried more than thirty feet into the beach to support a concrete mat that is fully five feet thick.

STAGE HARBOR LIGHT *had a covered walk between the dwelling and the light tower, which was typical of many lighthouse stations.*

Once again, the fragile spit of land that's charted as Great Point is in danger of being almost fully washed away. Should Great Point itself disappear altogether, the lighthouse has now been designed to serve as an offshore light, not unlike the one at Cleveland Ledge. In doing this, the engineers have planned for Great Point Light to have a lifecycle of one hundred years.

By then, perhaps, all the other towers along these shores might well have disappeared through lack of need and lack of any reason to retain them. Surely, no other lights will ever be built like those which once had

GREAT POINT LIGHT *is now supported by this new tower with solar panels.*

welcomed the black Atlantic nights and the seamen who sailed in such darkness. Yet, it is hard to imagine that this shore once stood absolutely dark.

Shallow and swift and soft as sand, the land of Cape Cod, Nantucket, and Martha's Vineyard can still sweep low and weak beneath the rushing combers. Those who know the Cape & Islands now will say these emotions are true. And yet the sailors of the early times knew none of this at all. In this respect, at

BUTLER FLATS LIGHT, *just off historic Fairhaven, marks the entrance to New Bedford. Though built upon a caisson, it has always been as fully-equipped as any station upon a coastal foundation.*

BUTLER FLATS
1898: Buzzards Bay, New Bedford
WHITE TOWER UPON CAISSON IN CHANNEL
Flashes white every 4 seconds
RANGE: 4 MILES

From Mattapoisett, take Route 6 west to New Bedford and watch for Cove Street. Follow it to *Davy's* overlooking Butler Flats; the ferry pier is nearby.

For passage through New Bedford Harbor, see the *Transportation Appendix.*

BUZZARDS BAY PLATFORM
was America's first aid to naviga-
tion based upon Gulf Coast oil rigs.

least, those mariners were no more certain than Columbus had been, and the only lights which once they had been certain of seeing were simply those they had imagined.

CLEVELAND LEDGE
1943: Buzzards Bay
STYLIZED WHITE TOWER
UPON A CAISSON
Flashes white every 10 seconds
RANGE: 17 MILES

With the exception of the reconstructed tower at Great Point on Nantucket, the lighthouse at Cleveland Ledge was the last to be commissioned and built anywhere in New England. Using engineering technology superior to that used at Minots Ledge or Bishop & Clerks, the lighthouse is set upon a submerged caisson in the waters of Buzzards Bay. It can only be reached either by private vessel, or by scheduled passage through Buzzards Bay.

For passage through Buzzards Bay, see the *Transportation Appendix.*

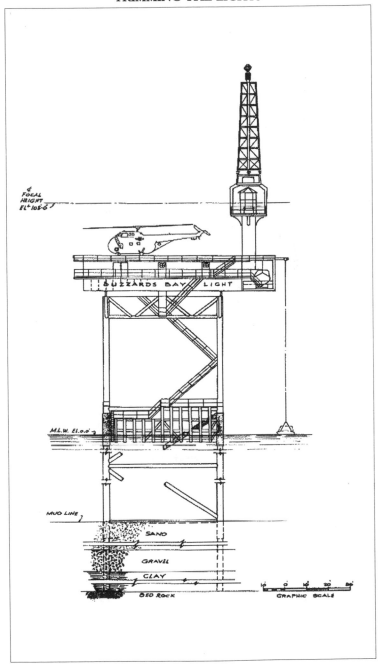

BUZZARDS BAY PLATFORM *replaced lightships* — VINEYARD SOUND, *as well as* HEN & CHICKENS — *that marked the approach to Buzzards Bay for more than 100 years. Two of a dozen that had protected local waters, the lightships were anchored in the sandy shallows where lighthouses could not be constructed.*

The Coast Guard Relief lightship is shown here leaving this post after the station was commissioned on November 1, 1966. The tower itself was the first such deepwater offshore light, and twenty-one others were planned for the ensuing decade to replace other lightships along America's shoreline.

As an eventual solution to their problems, though, the lighthouse has since been supplanted throughout the world. Along this crooked coast, the original stations of colonial America all were replaced in generations past, yet most of those replacement towers and the ones built since still stand along the coast. All but Boston Light have since been automated, and a few of these stations have been abandoned by the government altogether. Given that less than a dozen lights were commissioned throughout New England in the 20th century, their legions do not seem destined to grow.

Gone, are the lights built of local concern, and the schooners and clippers, as well as fish that lured fishermen here. Gone, too, are the wicks and the "wickies" alike.

Still, it remains doubtful that any of those selfless souls might understand any way of guiding a ship other than by the loom of light that once had been their way of life. And which once marked the safest passage through this part of the world. ⚓

146

TRANSPORTATION APPENDIX

FLIGHT SERVICE

Cape Cod

BARNSTABLE AIRPORT/Hyannis
508-775-2020
Commercial airlines to Boston, Martha's Vineyard, Nantucket, New Bedford.

CAPE COD AIRPORT/Marstons Mills
508-428-8732
Private and charter flights.

CHATHAM MUNICIPAL AIRPORT/Chatham
508-945-9000
Private and charter flights.

PROVINCETOWN AIRPORT/Provincetown
508-487-0241
Commercial airlines to Boston, Martha's Vineyard, and Nantucket.

Martha's Vineyard

KATAMA AIRFIELD/Edgartown
508-627-9018
Private and charter flights.

MARTHA'S VINEYARD AIRPORT/Edgartown
508-693-4776
Commercial airlines to Boston, Hyannis, Nantucket, and New Bedford.

Nantucket

NANTUCKET MEMORIAL AIRPORT/Nantucket
508-228-1255
Commercial airlines to Boston, Hyannis, Martha's Vineyard, New Bedford, and Provincetown.

New Bedford

ISLAND SHUTTLE/New Bedford
508-997-4095
Seaplane to Cuttyhunk.

Plymouth

PLYMOUTH AIRPORT/Plymouth
508-746-9326
Private and charter flights.

FERRY SERVICE

BAY STATE PROVINCETOWN CRUISES/Boston
617-723-7800
Seasonal service between Boston and Provincetown.

CAPE COD MUSEUM OF NATURAL HISTORY/Brewster
508-896-3867
Tours and overnight stays at Monomoy Point Lighthouse.

CAPE & ISLANDS EXPRESS/New Bedford
508-997-1688
Seasonal from New Bedford to Martha's Vineyard.
Year-round from New Bedford to Cuttyhunk.

FALMOUTH FERRY SERVICE/Falmouth
508-548-9400
Seasonal to Edgartown.

FREEDOM CRUISE LINE/Harwich Port
508-432-8999
Seasonal to Nantucket.

HY-LINE/Hyannis
508-775-7185
Harbor tours; year-round to Nantucket; seasonal to Martha's Vineyard.

ISLAND QUEEN/Falmouth
508-548-4800
Seasonal to Martha's Vineyard, the Elizabeth Islands, and through Buzzards Bay to the Cape Cod Canal.

TRANSPORTATION APPENDIX

MASSACHUSETTS AUDUBON SOCIETY/Wellfleet
508-349-2615
Seasonal tours of Elizabeth Islands.

MONOMOY NATIONAL WILDLIFE REFUGE/Chatham
508-945-0594
Tours of Monomoy Island.

ON TIME FERRY/Edgartown
508-627-9794
Service between Edgartown and Chappaquiddick.

PATRIOT PARTY BOATS/Falmouth
508-548-2626
Annual sunset Lighthouse Tour during Cape Maritime Week.

PLYMOUTH & PROVINCETOWN STEAMSHIP COMPANY/
Provincetown
508-487-2274
Seasonal route from Plymouth to Provincetown.

WOODS HOLE, MARTHA'S VINEYARD & NANTUCKET
STEAMSHIP AUTHORITY/Hyannis
508-540-2022
Year-round from Hyannis to Nantucket.
Year-round from Woods Hole to Martha's Vineyard.
Seasonal from Martha's Vineyard to Nantucket.

SANKATY HEAD LIGHT
*has always been vulnerable to
the same majestic waters that
threaten the Cape lights upon
the mainland to the north.*

Island
of
NANTUCKET

Drawn by Wᵐ. Coffin

For Macy's History of Nantucket.

1835.

THE LIGHTHOUSE PRESERVATION SOCIETY is a nonprofit organization dedicated to saving America's lighthouses. Their charter is to preserve historic lighthouse structures for future generations, to document their history, as well as that of their keepers, and to discover creative ways of making them more accessible to those who appreciate their heritage.

The recipient of the prestigious Presidential Achievement Award, the society continues to be both a highly effective national advocate and an enduring service provider to lighthouse preservation projects throughout the country. Its widespread public awareness campaign has generated some three million dollar in federal seed money for local preservation projects, initiated projects that demonstrate the adaptive reuse of these historic structures, and has assisted local groups across the nation with fundraising and technical advice.

In recent years the Lighthouse Preservation Society has proposed with success the Congressional estab-

NANTUCKET BEACON *is depicted inside the harbor on this rare chart from Obed Macy's* History of Nantucket. *Not indicated, though, are either the so-called "cliff lights" that were along the beach just north and west of* BRANT POINT, *or the light out at* SANKATY HEAD, *all built after Macy's history was published.*

lishment of a three-year Bicentennial Lighthouse Fund of federal matching grants for restoration projects; the proclamation of National Lighthouse Day; the nomination of ten lighthouse stamps for the United States Postal Service; and two national conferences in Washington, D.C. on the subject of preservation issues. More closely related to the lighthouses that surround Cape Cod, Nantucket & Martha's Vineyard, the society successfully proposed that the Great and General Court of Massachusetts enact a two million dollar Massachusetts Lighthouse Grants Program and that demonstration projects be initiated at several lighthouse sites, including Monomoy Point.

In addition, the society continues to raise funds for and to offer technical assistance to local groups on National Register nominations, research, relighting, Coast Guard leases, erosion control, exhibits, and other matters related to the preservation of our nation's lighthouses.

THE LIGHTHOUSE PRESERVATION SOCIETY
4 Middle Street
Newburyport, Massachusetts 01950 USA
1-800-727-BEAM

POINT GAMMON LIGHT,
*with its surrounding land
cleared, overlooks the distant*
BISHOP & CLERKS.

152

BIBLIOGRAPHY &
PHOTOGRAPHY CREDITS

Adams, Edward P. "Lighthouses and their Keepers." SCIENTIFIC
AMERICAN, (December 16, 1893).

Adamson, Hans Christian. KEEPERS OF THE LIGHTS. New York:
Greenberg (1955).

Allen, Everett S. A WIND TO SHAKE THE WORLD. Boston:
Little, Brown & Company.

Anderson, W.P. "Lighthouse Illuminants," SCIENCE, Volume 21
(May 12, 1893).

Anonymous. "The Highland Light," THE ATLANTIC MONTHLY,
Volume 14, Number 86 (December, 1864).

Anonymous. "Lighthouses, Lightships, and Buoys," SCIENTIFIC
AMERICAN, Volume 67 (September 10, 1892).

Anonymous. "Lighthouse Illuminants," SCIENCE, Volume 16
(November 14, 1890).

Anonymous. "Lighthouse Illumination," SCIENTIFIC AMERICAN,
Volume 65 (June 11, 1892).

Burchard, John. THE ARCHITECTURE OF AMERICA: *A Social and
Cultural History*. Boston: Little, Brown & Company (1961).

Carse, Robert. KEEPERS OF THE LIGHTS: *A History of American
Lighthouses*. New York: Chas. Scribner's Sons (1969).

Chamberlain, Barbara. THESE FRAGILE OUTPOSTS: *A Geological
Look at Cape Cod, Martha's Vineyard, and Nantucket*. New York:
Doubleday & Company (1964).

Chase, Mary Ellen. THE STORY OF LIGHTHOUSES. New York:
W.W. Norton & Company (1965).

Chase, R.T. "Lighthouses." CAPE COD Magazine, (May, 1918).

Conklin, Irving. GUIDEPOSTS OF THE SEA. New York: MacMillan
(1939).

Cusack, Betty Bugbee. COLLECTOR'S LUCK: *A Thousand Years at
Lewis Bay, Cape Cod*. Stoneham, Ma: Barnstead Print (1967).

Deyo, Simeon L. HISTORY OF BARNSTABLE COUNTY,
MASSACHUSETTS. New York: H.W. Blake & Co. (1890).

Drake, Samuel G. BIOGRAPHY AND HISTORY OF THE INDIANS OF

AMERICA'S LANDFALL

NORTH AMERICA. Boston: The Antiquarian Institute (1837).

Heap, D.P. ANCIENT AND MODERN LIGHTHOUSES. Boston: Ticknor & Company (1889).

Heap, D.P. "Methods of Revolving the Optical Apparatus for Lighthouses," SCIENTIFIC AMERICAN, Volume 81 (November 25, 1899).

Holland, Francis Ross, Jr. AMERICA'S LIGHTHOUSES: *Their History Since 1716.* Brattleboro, Vt: Greene Press (1972).

Huden, John C. INDIAN PLACE NAMES OF NEW ENGLAND. New York: Museum of the American Indian Foundation (1962).

Johnson, Arnold B. THE MODERN AMERICAN LIGHTHOUSE SERVICE. Washington, D.C.: U.S. Gov't Printing Office (1890).

Kittredge, Henry C. CAPE COD: *Its People and Their History.* Boston: Houghton Mifflin Company (1968).

Kobbe, Gustav. "Life in a Lighthouse," CENTURY Magazine, Volume 47 (January, 1894).

Kobbe, Gustav. "Lighthouses and Their Keepers," SCIENTIFIC AMERICAN, Volume 69 (December 16, 1893).

Lawrence, C.A. "The Building of Minots Ledge Lighthouse," NEW ENGLAND Magazine, Volume 15 (October, 1896).

Macy, Obed. THE HISTORY OF NANTUCKET: *Being a Compendious Account of the First Settlement of the Island by the English together with the Rise and Progress of the Whale Fishery; and other historical facts relative to said island and its inhabitants in two parts.* Mansfield, Ma: Macy & Pratt (1880).

Morison, Samuel Eliot. ADMIRAL OF THE OCEAN SEA: *A Life of Christopher Columbus.* Boston: Houghton Mifflin (1942).

Nordoff, Charles. "The Lighthouses of the United States," HARPER'S Magazine, Volume 38 (January, 1913).

Pratt, Reverend Enoch. *A Comprehensive History , ecclesiastical and civil, of Eastham, Wellfleet and Orleans, County of Barnstable, Mass from 1644 to 1844.* (1844).

Putnam, George. LIGHTHOUSES AND LIGHTSHIPS OF THE UNITED STATES. New York: Houghton Mifflin (1917).

Putnam, George. "Beacons of the Sea," NATIONAL GEOGRAPHIC Magazine, Volume 24 (January, 1913).

Snow, Edward Rowe. FAMOUS LIGHTHOUSES OF NEW ENGLAND. Boston: The Yankee Publishing Company (1945).

Starbuck, Alexander. THE HISTORY OF NANTUCKET *(County, Island, and Town) including Genealogies of First Settlers.* Rutland, Vt: The Charles E. Tuttle Company (1969).

Thoreau, Henry David. CAPE COD. New York: W.W. Norton (1966).

Thompson, Frederic L. THE LIGHTSHIPS OF CAPE COD. Portland, Me: Congress Square Press (1983).

Trayser, Donald G. BARNSTABLE: THREE CENTURIES OF A CAPE COD TOWN. Hyannis, Ma: F.B. & F.P. Goss (1939).

Willoughby, Malcolm F. LIGHTHOUSES OF NEW ENGLAND. Boston: T.O. Metcalf Company (1929).

Witney, Dudley. THE LIGHTHOUSE. Boston: New York Graphic Society (1975).

ACKNOWLEDGMENTS & CREDITS

ii	*United States Coast Guard Archives*	Great Point Light
vi	*United States Coast Guard Archives*	Stage Harbor Light
xi	*National Archives*	Cape Cod Light
14	*Donald W. Davidson*	Nobska Light
17	*Donald W. Davidson*	Brant Point Light
18	*Collection of Robert Bates*	Beach Point Light
20	*Donald W. Davidson*	The Gurnet Light
23	*United States Coast Guard Archives*	The Gurnet Light
26	*Donald W. Davidson*	Nauset Light
28	*United States Coast Guard Archives*	Cape Cod Light
32	*United States Coast Guard Archives*	Cape Cod Light
33	*Collection of Robert Bates*	Cape Cod Light
35	*United States Coast Guard Archives*	Gay Head Light
36	*United States Coast Guard Archives*	Gay Head Light
37	*United States Coast Guard Archives*	Cape Cod Light
38	*United States Coast Guard Archives*	Cape Pogue Light
40	*United States Coast Guard Archives*	Cape Pogue Light
41	*National Archives*	Fog signal illustration
42	*United States Coast Guard Archives*	Chatham Light
45	*United States Coast Guard Archives*	Chatham Twin Lights
46	*United States Coast Guard Archives*	Race Point Light
49	*Donald W. Davidson*	Scituate Harbor Light
51	*United States Coast Guard Archives*	Race Point Light
52	*United States Coast Guard Archives*	Tarpaulin Cove Light
55	*Donald W. Davidson*	Point Gammon Light
57	*United States Coast Guard Archives*	Minots Light air vent
60	*United States Coast Guard Archives*	West Chop Light
63	*United States Coast Guard Archives*	West Chop Light
64	*Donald W. Davidson*	West Chop Light
65	*United States Coast Guard Archives*	Bird Island Light
66	*United States Coast Guard Archives*	Bird Island Light
68	*United States Coast Guard Archives*	Monomoy Point Light
71	*The Lighthouse Preservation Society*	Billingsgate Light
73	*United States Coast Guard Archives*	Nauset Light
76	*United States Coast Guard Archives*	Three Sisters Lights
77	*Donald W. Davidson*	Three Sisters Lights
78	*United States Coast Guard Archives*	Cuttyhunk Light
81	*United States Coast Guard Archives*	Long Point Light
83	*United States Coast Guard Archives*	Long Point Light
84	*Donald W. Davidson*	Edgartown Harbor Light
85	*United States Coast Guard Archives*	Minots Ledge Light
87	*National Archives*	Minots Ledge Light illustration
89	*United States Coast Guard Archives*	Edgartown Harbor Light
91	*United States Coast Guard Archives*	Dumpling Rock Light
92	*United States Coast Guard Archives*	Cape Cod beacons
95	*United States Coast Guard Archives*	Nobska Light (top)
	Collection of Andrew Scherding	Nobska Light (bottom)
97	*United States Coast Guard Archives*	Ned Point

INDEX

— E —

East Chop Light 62, *108,* 109, 138, *139*
eclipser 96, 98-9
Eddystone Light 86
Edgartown Harbor Light *84,* 85, 88, *89*
Elizabeth Islands 25, 30
Emerson, Ralph Waldo x
English Channel 65
erosion 43

— F —

Fifth Auditor of the Treasury 64*ff,* 88, 129
fishery 39*ff*
fog 31, 56-8
fog signal *41,* 61, *65*
Fresnel, Augustin 105
Fresnel lens *37, 107,* 109, *123*
Friends of Sankaty Head 138

— G —

Ganteaume & McMullen Architects 142*ff*
Gay Head Light 34, *35, 37,* 65, 67, 76, 90, 93, 107
geographic range 77
glacier 43, 105
global positioning systems (GPS) 134
Gosnold, Bartholomew 22, 25, 65
Great Outer Beach 18, 27, 43, 57, *59,* 72
Great Point 35, 58, *59*
Great Point Light *ii, xii,* 4, 24, 140*ff, 142*
Groves, Jens Pedersen 43
Gulf of Maine 29
Gulf Stream 30, 31, 44
Gurnet Light *20,* 21, 22, *23,* 45, 58-9

— H —

Hallett, Daniel Snow
Hamilton, Alexander 64
Hen & Chickens Lightship *146*
High Lands 17, 27, 44
Highland Light (*see* Cape Cod Light)
Hinckley, Capt. Charles 120
Holmes Hole (*see* Vineyard Haven)
Hull 35
Hyannis Harbor Light 112
hydraulic lamp

— I —

Ipswich 85

— J —

Jones, Christopher 44-5
Judas lantern ix

— K —

keepers 119*ff*

— L —

Labrador Current 29
landfall ix, 15
lens order 105
Lewis, Capt. Winslow 67, 101-102, 109
Lighthouse Board 88-9, 129
Lighthouse Inn 125, 137
Lighthouse Preservation Society 138, 160
lightning rod 51, 57, 129
lightships 137, 143-6
Little Brewster Island 19, 54
Long Point Light 45, *81,* 82, *83*
loom 15
LORAN 134
luminous range 83

— M —

malle barre 25

158

This nautical chart of waters surrounding
Cape Cod, Nantucket & Martha's Vineyard
is a section of the
GENERAL CHART OF THE COAST No. VII
CAPE ANN TO BLOCK ISLAND
WITH GEORGES BANK,
published November of 1892 by the
United States Coast and Geodetic Survey,
T.C. Mendenhall, Superintendent.